LONE SURVIVOR
Judge, Jury, and Executioner

Louis Bernard Antoine, M.D.

Reggie,
One day, Haiti
will rise up
back to greatness
again!...
L B Antoine MD
1/28/99

VANTAGE PRESS
New York

All characters and events in the following story are fictional. Any resemblance to actual events or people who might exist (or existed) is purely coincidental.

FIRST EDITION

Published by Vantage Press, Inc.
516 West 34th Street, New York, New York 10001

Manufactured in the United States of America
ISBN: 0-533-12846-3

Library of Congress Catalog Card No.: 98-90590

0 9 8 7 6 5 4 3 2 1

In memoriam of **Reverend Jean-Marie Vincent,** who was my "chef d'equipe" at the Petit Seminaire, College St. Martial. He was taken away from us prematurely because he dared to stand for what he believed in. He dedicated his life to the struggle of the people and yet he never sought glory for himself. . . .

In memoriam of **Antoine Izmery,** who showed courage to the very end. He dared to play a different tune from that of those who have dominated Haiti from the beginning. . . .

In memoriam of the thousands of unknown victims of the bloodiest coup in Haitian history. . . .

Let us hope that their blood, and that of all those before them—Jacques Stephen Alexis, Gasner Raymond, Richard Brisson—was not spilled in vain. May it be the seed that sprouts peace, freedom, and justice from the soil of Haiti, for all Haitians who still claim the beleaguered country as their fatherland. . . .

Qu'est-ce que le Tiers Etat? ***Tout.***

Qu'a-t-il été jusqu'à présent dans l'ordre politique? ***Rien.***

Que demande-t-il? ***A y devenir quelque chose.***

What is the Third Estate?[1] ***Everything.***

What has it been until now in the political order? ***Nothing.***

What is its demand? ***To become something in it.***

Qu'est-ce que le Tiers Etat?
—Emmanuel-Joseph Sieyes (1789)

[1] The masses.

Contents

Introduction

It is the dream of every man that when the bell tolls, he will stand ready to face his destiny and resist any attempts by fellow men to destroy his humanity.

It is the dream of every man that when confronted with seemingly insurmountable challenges, he will reach within himself for untapped strengths and emerge victorious.

It is the dream of every man to be the hero who saves the day and causes the forces of good to prevail over the forces of evil.

Every era, every generation seems to produce only a few such men. They seem to be hand picked by the gods, groomed with care, and endowed with all the tools necessary to save the world from slipping back into the Dark Ages.

Ronald Benjamin St. Fort (aka Ben-X) was such a man. Possessing an indomitable character, he was courageous, versatile, and athletic. He was a man of superior intelligence. Victimized many a time, but never defeated. Like a combat-tested warrior, he had the ability to withstand tremendous physical and emotional challenges. Athletic, graceful, and handsome, he had the charisma of an African king. So when, in 1991, Haiti was thrust into the abyss of death and impending annihilation, it was a call to duty for Ben-X. He could not remain passive while his country was forced back into servitude. The small island nation was part of the whole world, part of the human race. Any time a human being was mistreated, humanity was destroyed. Ben-X was determined to stand up and do something. The lone survivor of the massacre of his family, persecuted by a rogue army set on destroying him, he would go underground until he was ready to return and seek justice . . . single-handedly.

He is the lone survivor. He is judge, jury, and executioner. Ben-X is our superhero. Long live Ben-X.

Part One

In the Name of the Constitution or in the Name of the Status Quo?

O freedom, what crimes are committed in thy name!
—Jeanne Manon Roland

1

Port-au-Prince, Haiti, circa 1991, Day One

8:00 A.M.: Place de L'independence

"Ratata . . . ta tatata ta ta . . . ratata ta ratata . . ."

Bullets were exploding everywhere. The rapid succession of shots from the automatic weapons was persistent. *Oh, no, not again!* seemed to be the expression on the faces of the early morning pedestrians, as they hurriedly tried to clear the streets. It had been more than fifteen minutes, and the shooting still had not stopped. What could possibly be happening? A major event must be unfolding.

The armored vehicles from the Army Headquarters were on the move. The soldiers from the infantry division had donned their fatigues and combat gear. It had been just another day in Port-au-Prince until the city's morning routines were disturbed by the gunshot sounds. The pristine beauty of the cobalt blue Caribbean sky announced that morning was breaking. The sun was already high and warming the hearts and spirits of the early risers. Port-au-Prince was fully awake. The colorful tap-taps had completed several runs, moving the commuters to wherever their destinations would be that day. The national anthem had played on the radio, and the red and blue flag was gracefully spangling over the immaculate and recently refurbished *Palais National.*

Less than a mile away, the Army Headquarters was unusually active that morning. The off-white two-story building, with a wide balcony encircling the structure, served as the center of operations for a 7,000-man army that consumed close to 60 percent of the gross national product. No serious activities usually took place there until about eleven o'clock in the morning. It was then that the high ranking officers, sporting impeccable khaki uniforms, made their grand entrances as their subordinates, vying for recognition, shouted, "Attention." The guards would raise their rifles in salute while the pleased officers, strutting like peacocks, would simply reply, "As you were," and proceed to their bunkers to attend to the business of the day.

The large balcony that surrounded the building had often served as an observation post for the high-ranking officers. They liked to watch over the crowds dancing to the beat of the latest carnival tune. Often they would simply loaf around until their official business or the baking heat of the Caribbean sun chased them back to their air-conditioned offices. It is an important business to run an army that gives refuge to gamblers and loan sharks.

The Haitian Army's latest edition had been assembled in the early decades of the century by the United States's occupying force and had not significantly changed in fifty years. In the early seventies, the first act of a newly selected president for life, Baby Doc, was to reopen the *Academie Militaire.* It is believed that the moguls of the Duvalier regime were asked to contribute their sons to be members of the first promotion of officers: the Class of 1971–1973. Many parents considered it a once in a lifetime opportunity for their families to enter into the elite class. To them, it was a dynasty with unlimited financial possibilities. However, there were scholastic requirements. Naturally, a large number of official documents were forged—no diploma or parchment was going to get in the way of such a historic call to duty.

The premier class of the *Academie Militaire* was formed. The group, composed of loyal Duvalierists, would dominate the Haitian political arena for decades. The change of the guards was ensured for years to come. Presently, the members of that group were well entrenched in the upper echelons of the Armed Forces. Attempts had been made at improving the combat readiness of an army that rarely saw any action. The most serious attempt at polishing the image of the army was made during the latter years of the Duvalier regime, with the creation of *"Le Corps des Leopards."* It is reported that a visiting dignitary from the American government had pressed the former dictator for reforms. The dictator, as he often did, quickly summoned his troops and brought in militia men and peasants by the truckloads to parade upon the lawn of the *Palais National*.

Unimpressed, the American official quipped, "Is it with these puppets that you plan to fight the communists?"

"Well, maybe the representative from the sister nation wants to help us build an elite corps to do the job," the president, famous for his shrewdness, retorted. Papa Doc was not going to pass up such a golden opportunity to pick the pocket of his feisty guest.

A few months later, the *Corps des Leopards* was born. It was touted as the elite force—the jewel of the Haitian Army—with a sacred mission to protect the gains of the *Revolution*. Its members were known for their viciousness, but much more for their lack of discipline, incompetence, and cowardice. What they learned best, perhaps, was how to hide at the first sign of a conflict. It was difficult for them to behave any differently, for the only time they were called to action was against unarmed civilians of their own country. The Haitian Army's reputation had not changed much after fifty years. To characterize this army, one could look to the writings of Machiavelli: "They are brave among friends; among enemies they are cowards." They loved being soldiers during peacetime, but in times of war, they either deserted or departed. Folk-singer-turned-politician, Manno Charlenajne, so aptly described them with the words:

> Ki sa nou rele you enemi, nan you sosyete ki defini chak klas avek you jan de vi?
> Fok nou kapab analize you pouriti pou sa li ye . . .
> Se sak kap kraze-n pou nou kap viv san limanite
> Nan you sosyete ki dwe chanje . . . *

> Who do we call our enemies, in a society that defines each class with a lifestyle?
> One must be able to define rottenness for what it is . . .
> Our real enemies are the ones who are destroying us, so we could live without humanity (and dignity) in a society that must change . . .

In Haiti, where unemployment and underemployment were rampant, the army had been the largest source of jobs in a nation barely the size of Maryland. In a country where the majority of the citizens could neither read nor write, one need only give a semi-literate man a rifle and a uniform. Next, inculcate into his head the idea that he is superior to his civilian fellow citizens. Tell him that he *is* above

*Used by permission of Joseph Emmanuel Charlemagne.

the law . . . because he is the law. Should the bug of presidential candidacy bite you, a mere civilian, fall on your knees and beg him to support you. Flatter him. Shower him with praise. Tell him how impressed you are with his statuesque demeanor, his gracefulness, and his pageantry. Tell him that when he is reviewing his troops in his flawless uniform, he is *like Capois La Mort* facing the enemy. Equate him to the founders of Haiti: Toussaint Louverture, Jean-Jacques Dessalines, and Henri Christophe. Isn't it the dream of every military man to see his picture in the history books amongst the heroes, the forefathers of the nation? Place him right there. Make it very convincing. You will be surprised how easy it is to have him believe you. Your ability to recognize his greatness can only be a testimony to how smart you are. The seeds you sow will fall on fertile ground. He was predestined to be great and you are but the lowly messenger. If you are a member of the aristocracy or the bourgeoisie, offer this man your virgin daughters, share your wife with him, and invite him to your dinner table. Serve him your best cognac, and flatter his palate with your expensive imported wines. Tell him how handsome he is. Take him for a stroll in the garden of your bucolic mansion while savoring Beethoven's *Ninth Symphony.* Tell him that his grace equals that of an African king. If that is not enough, tell him that he is the air that makes the whole country breathe. Introduce him to your friends as the peacock of the town. Anoint him with the scented oil of aristocracy. Stamp him with the coveted seal that will serve as irrefutable proof that he has finally arrived. He has made it into the privileged class of the *nouveaux riches.* Go gaga over his sexual prowess. Go ahead; do not hesitate. You will get your money's worth. Your downtown business will blossom. When you became an ally of such a powerful man, which peon, which civil servant in customs would dare get in the way of your shady transactions? It is just a case of one smuggler helping another. Isn't that what friends are for?

After you have done all of that, take a good look at what you have. You have just created a demi-god . . . a monster . . . an egomaniac. You have just created a Haitian military man . . . a coup maker . . . a putschist. You have created a unique class of person who bears comparison to no one. A citizen with his own rules, his own code of ethics. A person who will blindly follow orders to kill his neighbors—even his own mother. You have created a man without a moral conscience . . . a friend to no one. Like St. Peter did to Christ, he will deny that he even knows the ghetto from which he came. But everyone knows. You have created a *san manman*[1], a man *sans foi ni loi*[2] who will not hesitate to do anything to achieve his ends. You have created a man whose only allegiance is to his immediate superior: the one person who can make or break him. For, with every promotion he receives within that corrupted system, the military man is better positioned to steal, pluck, plunder, wheel, deal, rape, smuggle, traffic, and amass a fortune in no time. Not to mention the fact that he is a prime target for recruitment by a foreign intelligence agency.

You have just cloned Brigadier General Tobias, Lieutenant Colonel Franklin, and the like. Seven thousand of them, to be more exact. Multiple a meager monthly captain's salary of $160 U.S. by thirty-six months. What do you get? About $5,800 over three years, right? Wrong! Not in the Haitian Army. In the Haitian Army, the answer to this simple multiplication is millions of dollars. Three years . . . that is all it takes for that certain army officer to become a millionaire. If you have any doubt about the person with whom you are dealing, go and ask him yourself. He does not think that he is stealing. He does not think that he is immoral. Not even Machiavelli, the master of political pragmatism, could have seen any glory for such a man. For it was he who wrote, "Still, it cannot be called skill [*virtú*] to kill one's fellow citizens, to betray friends, to be without faith, without mercy, without religion; by these means one can acquire power but not glory."[3] However, glory was hardly the primary goal of the Haitian military man.

The first and foremost task of this army was to make money. The military officers were there to continue a tradition. What could possibly be wrong with continuing a tradition? Isn't the Haitian Army all about tradition? Of course, the uniformed men would entertain you with the idea that they were there only to perpetuate the army's glorious past. They would not hesitate to bring up the names of revered Haitian military men such as General Laveaux, Alexandre Petion, and Pierre Sully Guerrier. The difference, among others, is that those men had to face real danger—they had to fight real enemies. Real bullets were fired at them.

There has always been a love/hate relationship between the army and the Haitian people. Like a woman who is involved in an abusive relationship with her husband, the Haitian people keep returning and continue to show their fascination with the military man. It seems that the Haitian people never get enough of the pageantry. You can always count on a military parade and concerts of military marches to draw a crowd. The blows, the betrayals, and the clandestine deals are quickly forgotten. Friendship with a member of the army is something to be valued and cherished. After all, in spite of everything, they are the Haitian people's brothers and fathers. The Haitian people will often rave about and exaggerate the nature of this relationship. For the most part, Haitians love their military men, the defenders of their country. *"L'état c'est moi,"* the famous words from the French King Louis XIV, could easily come from any one of them. His behavior is that of someone who owns the country and everything within it. Any questions?

In any organized nation, the role of the army is to maintain law and order and to safeguard the nation. In Haiti, the army has always striven on chaos, lawlessness, and exploitation. Such a situation is seen as a tremendous opportunity for the reshuffling of power and the riches that come with it. Just imagine if a newly elected president starts spreading the gospel of change, encouraging the military men to become more civic minded and actively involved in the socioeconomic development of the country. Naturally, this man automatically becomes the enemy of the Haitian Army. No matter how innocent his ideas might sound, if he dares to talk about changes, that's it. He is doomed. He is ipso facto earmarked for the next *coup d'état.* Whose turn is it to be president? The military man has lost track. For he has promised the *fauteuil presidentiel*[4] to so many presidential hopefuls. Imagine a father promising his daughter's hand in marriage to several men at the same time. This would be a very dishonorable thing to do in any civilized society. However, in Haiti, the rule of the jungle often prevails. As Jean de La Fontaine wrote in his fable "The Wolf and the Lamb," "La raison du plus fort est toujours la meilleure."[5] Let there be no doubt in anyone's mind who the stronger man is in Haiti.

Who had the Uzis, the grenade launchers, and the men trained to use them? The answer is obvious: the Haitian Army. This would not be a problem if the military men could be trusted to follow the orders of a civilian president, in accordance with the Constitution. In Haiti, trusting the Armed Forces could be a very risky and dangerous proposition. One is likely to be manipulated, stabbed in the back, and discarded when one no longer fits the army's needs of the moment. The army's deeds had always been guided not by honor, but by expediency and the smell of money. The saddest part of it all is that the generals could hide behind their carefully designed public images while the enlisted men carried out the dirty job of massacring the Haitian people. What irony. The *Ti solda* (enlisted men) would casually shoot people in the slums and then return to the same neighborhoods when off duty. These same soldiers came from the masses and would have been among the first to benefit from a changed society. On payday, they are considered lucky if they take home a few dollars. Creditors and loan sharks within the army itself very often garnish their stipends. They have been brainwashed into believing that they belong to a special class within the Haitian society: a class that does not have to abide by the basic rules of mutual respect and civility that bind the community.

Notes

1. Hooligan.
2. Without faith, without law.
3, Machiavelli's *The Prince,* in reference to Agathocle, the tyrant of Syracuse.
4. Presidential seat.
5. "The stronger man's reasoning always carries the day."

2

This was the army that Jean Bernard Alexandre was counting on to safeguard his presidency. The fate of Jean Bernard Alexandre was, therefore, sealed very early in his presidency. He was never in full command of the Haitian Army. Democracy, embodied in its new president, was on probation in the beleaguered nation. Jean Bernard Alexandre's probation period was over. He was found unfit for the job by the ones who beared the bayonets.

A few key officers are concentrated in the area surrounding the *Place de L'independence (Champ de Mars)*. It is an area not larger than a few square miles. Besides the *Palais National* and the general headquarters, there are the American Consulate, the main military barracks, and several hotels frequented by foreign journalists. This area was, in essence, the nerve center of the country—the command post from which all important decisions were made. Well, almost all. Some were made in other countries' embassies. When shots of heavy artillery rang that morning, everyone knew that something big was happening. These were not gunshots between the usual cops and robbers. Nor were they the kind that occur when two hotheaded macho men try to settle a score. These were heavy artillery shots . . . small cannon shots with bullets nearly the size of a cucumber. The shots were coming from the Army Headquarters. They were aimed at the *Palais National,* the symbol of the presidency. It had been thirty-three years since shots had been fired from a military building toward the official residence of the president. History was repeating itself.

Was there a mutiny in the ranks of the Forces Armées d'Haiti (FAD'H)? A few rebellious soldiers shooting at the residence of their commander in chief? No; it was yet another episode of a much deeper conflict. The saga continues. The Haitian Army was at it again. The men in uniform, who held the rifles and the bayonets, were once more refusing to submit to civilian authority. The army once again was ready to play its favorite role of broker between the different factions of the civilian society. Or possibly the army, tired of the squabble, holds onto the coveted prize all for itself.

It is true that the rhetoric from the Duvalierists on Radio Liberte had become much louder and more daring every day. It is true that the eccentric host, Richelieu, had captivated the listening audience with his flowery comments. And only a few days earlier, in front of the United Nations, the president had astonished the world with his oratory talents. It was also true that the pseudo-bourgeoisie of Port-au-Prince had felt directly targeted by a speech delivered by Jean Bernard Alexandre. But another coup? Hadn't the country been down that route less than ten months before? Hadn't the masses taken to the streets and forced the Duvalierists to retreat in an unprecedented show of popular resolve? Another coup? Hadn't the superpowers committed millions of dollars to the establishment of democracy in Haiti? Or were the superpowers so displeased with the outcome of the election that they wanted to renege on their much-touted experimentation with democracy? Imagine a bully playing cards with some friends. He suddenly realizes that his hand of cards is not so great. What does he do? He pulls his nine-millimeter gun and orders, with a threatening voice, "Reshuffle the cards!" That is what the Haitian Army and its backers from the so-called civilized world had just done. Forget about the rules. Forget about the Constitution. Isn't the army supposed to defend its country and its people from all enemies? So, what happened here? Well, in Haiti anything is possible. You raise a few million dollars . . . you pledge allegiance to the star spangled banner. You might even get the help of a sophisticated Intelligence Agency to create a phony dossier on the president you want to overthrow. Big brother will see no evil, hear no evil. Voila! It is a done deal. The *coup* is complete. Next? Who wants to be the *president du jour?* Be careful with that question. You might create a traffic jam in front of the Army General Headquarters. Every pseudo-intellectual, every banker, social worker, or physician could come up with some very good reasons why he feels he is the best candidate for the job. He might tell you in confidence of the dream he had the night before or the secret revealed to him by his houngan (voodoo priest). "I see you wearing a long redingote[1] with a red and blue sash over your shoulder. You are sitting among dignitaries from all over the world. A *Te Deum* is being played in your honor. Outside of the National Cathedral, an army battalion is waiting to be reviewed by you, Your Excellency. The military band is playing *La Dessalinienne*. Oh! That wide smile on your face. You have finally arrived. Your rendezvous with greatness has finally been accomplished." Such a divination from the voodoo priest was all the confirmation that the exalted "president to be" needed. For he has always known that one day he would rise above the commoners, respond to the call of duty, and face his great destiny. He has already begun to prepare his inaugural address. Oh that deadly disease of "presidentitis" that has plagued the majority of Haiti's intellectuals. What a disease! Now that the intellectual has heard it from the man who can communicate with the gods, the voodoo priest, nothing can stop him. Every one of his moves, every one of his meetings will be geared toward that phantasm. In the morning, before he leaves his home, he will piously consult with the gods and make his offerings. One never knows. Pray to all the gods. Because of this folly, nothing that any politician does can ever be right. He will not commit to any projects. He will never lay all his cards on the table. He will not use his skills for the service of the nation. The only job that he wants is to sign executive orders under the presidential seal and letterhead. No special skills needed. On the job training will be provided. Oh yes! Consultants from all walks of life and every nationality will flock all around him . . . for a price. Gifts will abound—it comes with the territory. In no time, the president will become rich. Pay is not based on merit. And if at first he does not succeed, he can always blame it on the opposition. It does not matter that his leadership qualities remain untested; his mind is set on the presidential seat.

The voodoo priest has spoken on behalf of the gods. It is a clear indication to proceed. The courting of the military man can now commence. Every pseudo-intellectual in this small country wants to be president. Never mind that he has not been able to manage the affairs of his family, to maintain gainful employment, or put food on the table for his wife and children. He now feels confident that he can manage a whole country. Is it any wonder that the one who holds the bayonet will always be a king maker, a holder of tremendous power? You never know when you might be called to fulfill your great destiny. No matter the cost in human lives! No matter the anguish brought on a whole nation! In this very way, on that fateful morning in September, another coup was, in fact, unfolding.

Yes, another coup! If the members of the Haitian Army could put an ad in one of the mercenary soldier magazines, it would probably read something like this:

> Do you want to overthrow a president?
> We have the men . . . we have the experience.
> We are the Haitian Army.
> Have guns and ammo, will shoot to kill!
> No job too small.
> References provided upon request.

Somebody should have told the Haitian people that their elected president was under attack. The element of surprise coupled with the viciousness of the military operations ensured the instantaneous success of the coup. In the dark of night, heavily armed military personnel cordoned off the most densely populated neighborhoods. When the army was ready to attack the presidential palace, there would be no outpouring of the masses on the streets. There would be no bonfires at the crossroads. This time, the army would take all necessary means to ensure the success of the operation. The people would not be able to run to the rescue of their beloved president. Some of them did try, however, and it cost them their lives. Close to 1,000 Haitians were killed in the hours following the coup. It was total confusion. The Haitian people were hit hard, extremely hard. It was as if a pair of forceps suddenly plunged into its chest and yanked its heart right out. All the Haitian people could do was to stumble to the ground stunned, lifeless.

It was not as if Haiti was suddenly stricken by a natural disaster like a volcano, a Noah-like flood, or a nuclear accident causing its disappearance from the surface of the globe. No, *this* was a mad-made disaster. The perpetrators? Haitians. It was a case of rape and incest all at once. Her very own children were violating Haiti. Throughout Haiti's history as a nation, her people had allied themselves with her enemies, spit in her face, forced her to the ground, stepped on her, and humiliated her. Was the country being invaded? Tanks and armored trucks were positioned around the *Palais National.* It was a country at war with its own self. The motive? The reason?

"I, only I, have the means and the knowledge to clean up the country's mess. In fact, I am so good that I will succeed where you and every leader before you have failed. I am, therefore, justified to forcefully depose or conspire to depose anyone who gets in the way. My turn has come. I have the historical duty to act. In other words, I am seizing the reins of power in order to save the country. I now have the right to dictate how the country is run. I now have if not the right, then the authority to direct the affairs of the state from the beautiful palace, a residence coveted by many, but inhabited by few."

His reasoning is fraught with *delusion de grandeur.* Such thinking always carries its cost in human lives, as it comes from vainglorious and deranged men. Their sense of duty is so inflated that the self-proclaimed Spartacuses will not hesitate to sacrifice thousands of human lives to turn a vision into a reality. Jews were exterminated by the millions. Black slaves were exterminated in comparable numbers (if not greater). In the events surrounding the *coup d'état,* Haitians died by the thousands. Unfortunately, it had become a common occurrence in Haiti. Some presidents took their sense of duty so seriously that they proclaimed themselves emperor, president for life, and "chef supreme et effectif des Forces Armées d'Haiti."[2] The previous dynasty had remained in power for thirty years. Once again, the army was set on wrestling the power away from the president.

The elected president has been ordered out. The marriage between the army and the executive branch, celebrated only seven months earlier in great fanfare, has abruptly ended. Cohabitation is no longer possible. What was wrong with this marriage? Everything. The president had his mind set on bringing about change; the army was determined to keep the status quo. The streets have been cleared. The population has been ordered to stay away. No one moves, nobody gets hurt. This is a stickup! Port-au-Prince is a giant crime scene. Somebody, please call the police! Not a chance, for the perpetrator *is* the police. Democracy is being brutally raped. The army is no longer taking orders from its commander in chief. Jean Bernard Alexandre, the symbol of this nascent democracy, is being insulted and threatened with death . . . he walks toward the Army Headquarters, holding his head high. Gunshots fly at him. He is undeterred. Maybe he could walk over and discuss the matter like gentlemen, with General Tobias. After all, as the president has often stated, they are brothers. Maybe they are, but so were Cain and Abel. So were Remus and Romulus. Yet, Romulus did not hesitate to kill his twin brother Remus when he founded Rome. One can never tell how far deep-rooted resentment and jealousy will take a man stricken with an inferiority complex. There seems to always be a need for comparison and challenge. Like two boys who suddenly discover their manhood and say to each other in the bathroom, "Mine is bigger than yours!"

"You should feel lucky to be alive," the strong man *du jour* states. In fact, a colonel has voted against ending the president's life. General Tobias looks very calm. He feels that he has the upper hand. He is almost toying with the president. Remember the words of Pontius Pilate: "So you are the king of the Jews." General Tobias states, "I am the chief of state now, and you are nothing. You are no longer the president." Just like that. It did not matter that this man was not just *any* man. It did not matter that Jean Bernard Alexandre competed with many candidates and came out victorious. This uniformed man was going to reverse the people's decision with impunity. Some other officers were acting more hostile. "Let's kill him and get it over with," they said. The president did not flinch. "What are you going to do now, kill the president?" asked Jean Bernard Alexandre. The French ambassador was present at the scene. Imagine the headlines: Army general in uniform kills elected president in cold blood in front of astounded diplomat. No! He did not have the guts. Under pressure from the French ambassador, the president's life is spared. The president of the republic, under heavy guard, is whisked away to the airport. The captain in charge of the presidential guard is ambushed and killed at close range. A nation is plunged back into the Dark Ages. A whole nation is suddenly vilified, humiliated.

The first black republic of the world has become the joke of every newscaster in the modern world. It has been a day of infamy; the day Haiti lost its innocence. The country will never be the same again. The tanks, left over from some rich country's surplus, roll out. The army is out in full gear, showing off its muscle. They have total control. The media are confused. The reports contradict each other. The official words: There has not been a coup. "It is only a democratic correction." It is both very tragic and comical for an army general to believe that he could treat a sovereign nation as homework. With a giant eraser, the general "corrected" the situation by committing treason.

Heavy artillery shots are fired at the *Palais National*. The president of the republic is being evicted from his official residence. He is forced to walk on foot to the Army Headquarters. Who is in charge here? Isn't the president supposed to be the commander-in-chief? Stop these imposters!

The perpetrators of the crime in progress are the police; the Haitian people are under a complete news blackout. The fate of their elected president is not known. Is he deposed or is he not? This masterful plan has Langley, Virginia, written all over it. The outside forces certainly did not want a repeat of earlier coup attempts when the masses took to the streets and the coup had to be aborted. No, these events were perfectly timed. The population was still half-asleep. There was a total blackout of news coverage. The usual trouble spots had no way of knowing what had taken place well after it had become irreversible.

It was a perfect coup. This time, the army had outdone itself. The army wanted to prove wrong the theory that in Haiti the military was just a refuge for rejects of society, the ones who could never make it in a competitive civilian society because they were less intelligent. There was a master strategist behind this coup. Whether or not the blueprint was conceived with the help of the CIA was irrelevant. The officers of the Haitian Army had executed it *sans bavure*.[3] If their aim was to seize control of the country no matter what the human cost, they had succeeded masterfully. Did they depart from the blueprint received from the boss from abroad by going overboard with the killings? Could such policy makers who seem nauseated and rightfully appalled when one drop of American blood is spilled on foreign soil go along with the extermination of thousands of human lives?

The obvious explanation was that as long as the victims were not Americans, the media would look the other way. In this case, the victims were black Haitians from a downtrodden, abjectly poor country, a country full of arrogance. Haiti had always been a constant reminder to everyone that the mightiest country of the planet had not been able to design a foreign policy that worked. A reminder of all the failed policies of the past, both a sore and a bad example. A country that every American government wished would just go away. Scram! Allez! Disappear! Ban-m talon-ou! So whether the Haitians died on the high seas or were massacred by their own brothers, who cares? Maybe the unconscious wish to see them disappear would come true. It is a commonly held belief that no coup can logistically take place in a small country like Haiti without the blessing of foreign agencies from the major countries. Had they given the green light this time too? Did they or didn't they know that Jean Bernard Alexandre was about to be toppled?

Brigadier General Tobias, it seemed, had lost a golden opportunity. He had a choice, a historical choice. He could have been a true brother to Jean Bernard Alexandre. He could have taken at least half of the credit in the creation of a society in which every Haitian would feel safe; where the rule of law would prevail. He could have built a country where Haitians could trust Haitians again. He had the choice to be the co-architect of a *shiny city on the hill*, a place called home where everyone would strive for the prosperity of all the citizens. A place where every adult would be treated with dignity, honor, and respect. A country where children would live with hope. This particular choice would have ensured him a life of glory and happiness among his Haitian brothers. Instead, General Tobias, with the complicity of his brothers in arms, chose to create a state of chaos, a dire hell where everyone lived in continuous fear and anxiety; a place where mothers and fathers were afraid that they might never see their children again. A country where you trusted your friends at your own risk. A place where hope and smiles have all but disappeared from the face of children who have lost their innocence. A place where it was no longer safe to take an evening stroll in the park. General Tobias chose, instead, to be haunted and tormented for the rest of his life by the disfigured faces and the ghosts of the fallen victims of his atrocities and his unleashed cruelty. He ensured himself an eternal reputation of shame and infamy. He committed a crime against humanity. Opprobrium will remain attached to his name wherever he goes. He will be remembered as the man who killed democracy. No amount of money will ever buy his peace. Every morning when he looks at himself in the mirror, he will have to admit, "I betrayed my people. I killed the hope of millions of people." Will he ever stand in front of the tribunal of history and acknowledge that, under his guard, thousands of innocent people were killed? Will he ever take responsibility for bringing terror and chaos to every Haitian family?

Notes

1. Fitted coat.
2. Supreme leader.
3. Without a hitch.

3

8:25 A.M.: Television Nationale

Flash! Breaking News!

"We interrupt this program to bring you the following news," Mr. Ravel started. "There are persisting rumors that another coup is in progress as we speak. *Manman pitit marre rin-nou.*[1] The armored cars are once again on the move . . ." The broadcast was suddenly interrupted. A group of well-armed men burst into the studio. The reporter was pulled out. A gun was placed to his head. He was ordered to get back in front of the camera and change the story he had started to report.

The action from the army was very swift. The military must have been in the neighborhood. Mr. Ravel was forced to do what every journalist fears the most: to make untrue statements under duress. Freedom of press had just become one of the very first victims of the coup. Mr. Ravel's life was spared for now because of his family relation with one of the new strong men in the town. Should he persist in creating panic by spreading subversive news, "the army could not guarantee that he and his family would be alive by the end of the day." Mr. Ravel could not have gotten a more direct message. He went into hiding and left the country soon thereafter. He was just one of the hundreds of thousands of displaced people. There were people moving all throughout the country. An estimated 300,000 people were displaced. They were refugees in their own country. Neighbors could no longer recognize their neighbors and, therefore, could not trust them. The darkest days of the Duvalier regime had returned.

10:00 A.M.: Police Headquarters, Downtown Port-au-Prince, Staff Meeting

Members Present: General Belizaire, nicknamed "The Brain," military academy laureate, former intern of a prestigious American military strategy school in Georgia. He is probably the most intelligent member of the whole Haitian Army. He does not like to show his face in public. He would rather plan, develop strategies, and advise behind the scenes. His travel itinerary included a visit to Washington, D.C. only a few weeks before the current events. He fell from grace during one of the many provisional governments in the immediate post-Duvalier era and was sent into exile. He may have spent some time in an American jail. Some believe that he was being punished for authoring perhaps the only coup in Haitian history to take place without the approval of his foreign bosses. Others believe it was a ploy and that, in fact, he was getting his CIA training and credentials. The plan was for him to be part of the cadre destined to rule Haiti with an iron fist. The events that followed his time abroad would indirectly confirm those rumors. Not only was he reinstated in the Haitian Army upon his return, but he was also promoted and became its most influential member.

General Belizaire was back with a vengeance. He quickly rose to the position of chief of staff. Whatever General Belizaire said was followed to the letter. Even as he gave his braggadocio speech stating what he would do to

Blan Meriken (white Americans), as Haitians like to call their powerful neighbors to the North, he was still on the CIA payroll. "You do not have to worry about *Blan Meriken* (Americans)," he said in one of his speeches. "If they ever set foot on the land of Haiti Thomas again, I will transform the land into a giant inferno." His words were very reminiscent of those of a famous military leader who proclaimed only days before his army was slaughtered, "Land battle is the mother of all battles." In a country where people seem to be very gullible, one could say anything. Such hyperbolic statements are so common among the Haitian Army officers that one would think it was part of their curriculum at the military academy. General Belizaire's bosses expected him to use such words as a cover for his clandestine involvement with the CIA.

General Cesar. Specialist: riot control and urban warfare. For many years, the dictatorial regime in Haiti lived in fear of popular uprising and the spread of guerilla warfare. The gap between the people living in indescribably miserable conditions and the filthy rich few was so profound that popular uprising seemed like a very distinct possibility. General Cesar's mission was to develop a master plan to deal with this eventuality.

He graduated second in his class at the military academy. His training took him to the infamous *Military School of the Americans* in Georgia—the school where most of the strong men and military dictators were groomed. General Cesar did extremely well there and was given a scholarship for further training at an American base in a NATO country. He speaks at least seven languages. He is probably the most refined member of the Haitian Army. He is an avid student of music history and world history. He looks out of place in this group of putschists.

He has independently maintained a large dossier on

the narcotics trade not just in Haiti, but in the whole Caribbean basin. Attempts by international drug enforcement agencies to recruit him have officially remained unsuccessful. How he has managed to remain uncompromised is a mystery. He has received many death threats but does not seem the least perturbed by them. The fact that he is still alive is a wonder in itself. After all, it was only fitting that he would be present at this momentous time to give posterity an accurate rendition of what really happened in the minds of the coup makers.

His favorite pastimes also include military marches and writing poetry. He has written a book about the atrocities of the American Occupation of Haiti from 1915 to 1934. Still, the question remains: What is he doing in the Haitian Army? He owns a large collection of paintings, military related memorabilia, and artifacts that could fill a whole wing of the National Museum. It is valued at several million dollars. He has taken his collection on international tours. He seems to be an aberration in this group of military men.

Lieutenant Colonel Michael Franklin: He rose within the ranks through his alleged connection with a drug cartel. It is said that he takes his orders only from his boss in Medellín, Columbia, and his section chief in the CIA. How he managed such cross training is beyond everyone. Reality or fiction, he seems perfect for the part, as he is extremely brave and will not stop at anything to get what he wants. He has the reputation of being a no nonsense officer. What Lieutenant Colonel Franklin wants, Lieutenant Colonel Franklin gets. Not bad for a country in which everything is left to chance. "The only predictable thing about Haiti," a famous journalist once said, "is that it is unpredictable." Lieutenant Colonel Franklin quickly understood that in Haiti, if you show enough guts, no one would dare challenge you on anything.

The rumors about this almost legendary figure are countless. Very soft spoken, he is believed to have an inferiority complex. He likes to portray himself as a man of duty. He is thought to be behind the *zenglendos*[2] who have been robbing houses and common citizens on the street. Of course, none of this has ever been confirmed, but in Haiti, rumors can ruin your reputation in a matter of days. The vivid nature of these rumors is such that they bring fear in one's heart at the mere mention of Lieutenant Colonel Franklin's name.

The firm would like to turn him loose, as his brazen ways have become a major concern. He has never shown much respect for the army's upper echelons, which is not at all surprising. As a child, he had no respect for authority figures. He was often expelled from school for disrupting the class and instigating fights with his peers. He received a three-week suspension once after he brought a live snake into the classroom and placed it on the chair of a frightened fourth grade teacher. His tenure in the army has not been any different so far. He has received many reprimand letters, but has always managed to be rescued at the last minute. Just when everyone is expecting him to get kicked out, along comes a telephone call from a higher power asking a baffled superior officer to back off.

It is widely believed that large sums of money have changed his superior's mind numerous times. He is a street fighter. There are no brawls too big for Lieutenant Colonel Franklin. He has gotten into numerous bar fights and has many scars to prove it. In any organized society, he would have been held accountable for not upholding the law. He was sent to New York on a scholarship, but spent most of his time partying. It is widely rumored that he once belonged to the *Bloods,* a violent gang from the New York

Metropolitan area. His parents started to worry about him becoming involved in criminal activities, so they used their connection with officials of Duvalier's regime to get him accepted into the military academy. He was an average student who would bet on everything. He even bet on his own score at the final exam. He rose through the ranks rather quickly and only a few years after graduation, he was a lieutenant colonel, owned hundreds of acres of land, and had his own private airfield strip. Within minutes of the events at the *Place de L'indépendence,* he gathered a few of his loyal followers, moved into the Police Headquarters, and declared himself chief of police. No one dared to challenge him. Chief of police it was. *Nollo contendere.*

Many other lower ranking officers were present. Colonel Gesner had traveled the whole night all the way from Port-de-Paix to make this meeting called in urgency in military codes over the army's modern communication system. Colonel Celestin, renowned for his gambling habits, owned half of the *borlete* banks around the country and was more interested in the impact of the unfolding events upon his lucrative business. He was officially stationed in Hinche, but spent most of his time in Port-au-Prince. He had to stay close to the action. Colonel Boursiquot should have lived in Germany during Hitler's reign. His specialty was interrogation. He had invented unimaginable torture techniques for retrieving information from his prisoners. His official post was in *Aux Cayes*. He was often summoned to Port-au-Prince to conduct questioning of important prisoners. It is believed that he was hand picked for this job by Papa Doc, himself, when he was only a sergeant. Representatives from the major military departments were present at the meeting, including Captain Marcelus, who remained half-asleep the whole time. They had been summoned to Port-au-Prince *quam primum*.

Members Absent: Brigadier General Tobias, commander a.i.: It is reported that he is still reluctant to join the movement as he feels indebted to Jean Bernard Alexandre for naming him commander. Others have it that he was more of a coward who took the army rules very seriously. His allegiance is to God, his country, and to his family, not necessarily in that order. No serious decision is made by this man without consulting with his Baptist pastor, his wife, and . . . his *mambo.* Contact with the voodoo priestess is usually made indirectly through his nanny, *Manze Jacqueline* (Miss Jacqueline), who has been with the family for many years. *Manze Jacqueline* could tell you countless secrets about this important man. She could tell you about his fear and trepidation when Jean Bernard Alexandre first made contact with the brigadier general. The powerful general was shaking like a leaf, wondering whether he was going to get promoted, transferred out, or simply given the boot. He made at least a dozen telephone calls before he obtained some confirmation that the meeting was going to be a good one. You see, politicians and high-ranking officers hardly ever leave their homes in the morning without consulting with some higher power, be it a houngan,[3] a Catholic priest, a pastor, or an advisor to the executive branch. They have to know from which direction the hurricane might be coming.

General Tobias had the face of an innocent man. One could easily give him Holy Communion without confession. His whole demeanor is so fake and so superficial that his subordinates laugh behind his back. He was perfect for the role of the reluctant leader who had to be convinced into the post in order to save his country from unruliness and civil war. He was able to fool many renowned journalists from major networks in America. General Tobias is a "very decent man who wants to see his country progress toward democracy." Move over Gerard Depardieu, there is a new movie star in town. From the outside he could easily be mistaken for a principled man whose word is golden. He plays dumb whenever he disagrees. He appears to be the cerebral type who rehashes things over and over before he renders an opinion. On the contrary: He has long made up his mind and, instead, spends much of the time worrying about his image. Conscious of his role as a commander, he is quite worried about how history will judge him. Therefore, he spends 10 percent of his time on substance and 90 percent on appearance. Maybe no one will understand why he has hired so many media and public relations consultants, including a full-fledged actor from Hollywood, a PhD, and a group of personal tailors. For Brigadier General Tobias, image is everything and much more. On approaching him more closely, one is quickly turned off by his similarity to a grazing cow. He will rehash things and ponder ad nauseam before he finally gives you some indication that he has got it. "Ah! That is what you mean," he'll say. You are fooled! Trust him at your own risk. One can never know where he stands on a subject. When he says yes, he means no. When he says no, he probably means yes or maybe. He does not trust anyone. Beware of his reactions!

Gerald Dubuisson, PhD: civilian advisor to the commander. How this man who used to profess revolutionary zeal ended up in this camp is a mystery to everyone. He was granted a scholarship to one of the best Ivy League universities in the United States. He knows the American political system inside out. No word comes out of the mouth of the brigadier general without Dubuisson's approval. He must make sure every speech and statement is politically correct, for the commander has to speak and walk like a statesman. Tobias thought that he might need the service of an *agent de liaison* with the civilian society and the international media. Yet how Dubuisson has managed to hold this position through four successive governments is a mystery to everyone. Maybe this highly educated man took his lead from Louis XIV courtiers, finding the right words to flatter those in positions of power. He can always be found in the front row of every official function. This time, he judged it very prudent to stay away from the meeting at the Police Headquarters. He wanted to make sure that he knew first which way the wind was blowing. He could always manipulate his way later, by concocting one of his brilliant political analyses of the situation. His role is not vastly different from the augur consultants of the pagan Roman empire. His tailor made gray suit, the Yves St. Laurent fitted shirt, and the 100 percent silk tie are de rigueur. He sits as an observer at every important meeting.

Summary of the Topics Discussed:

1: Crowd Control

"There are reports that masses from Cite Soileil, Bel-Air, Carrefour in Port-au-Prince, Raboteau in Gonaives, and Quatre-Chemins in Aux Cayes have been acting nervous and may take to the streets," the chief of information commented. "There cannot be any demonstration. The masses have to be controlled at all cost."

"General Belizaire, is there any contingency plan?" General Cesar asked.

"Of course," General Belizaire responded with enthusiam. "It will be up to the department and district commander that those *'va-nu-pieds'*[4]. do not take to the streets. All soldiers are on Condition 'D.' All vacation and personal leaves have been canceled. All the *ti solda*[5] are confined to their barracks. They have orders to 'shoot to kill' anything that budges after five-thirty tonight. They have orders to shoot if they feel like it. You get the point. The masses have to understand right away that we are not kidding. We mean business. We do not want to hear one word about this crazy priest."

"Are you sure all the soldiers will follow those orders?" General Cesar asked. "The president has a lot of supporters in some units."

"That is true," General Belizaire acquiesced, "but these soldiers have all been identified and we are ready to place them under arrest and move all of them to the national penitentiary."

2. Media control

It consists of a plan to develop and distribute a list of reporters, radio broadcasters, unions, and other popular organization leaders who are to be neutralized as quickly as possible. Some of the means include kidnapping, arresting, torturing, and even killing. One of the meeting attendees, Colonel Brunache, seemed to be uncomfortrable with the prospect of the butchery ahead. He asked with hesitation. "Do you mean that we will have to kill all of these people?"

"What do you think this is?" joked Lieutenant Colonel Franklin. "A Sunday choir rehearsal?"

"How about those damned jounalists? They are the ones who made that priest so damn popular. They are always making us look bad. That priest seems to do no wrong," cried General Ceasar in a high pitched and upset voice.

"Do not worry!" Lieutenant Colonel Michael Franklin commented. "As we speak, there is a little operation going on at Haiti-Inter, Radio Caraïbes, and Radio Tropics. They all will be sorry that they were even born."

Lientenant Colonel Franklin dominated the meeting. Close to an hour was spent discussing whether or not the members of the so-called *Brigades de Vigilance* should be included on the hit list. The *Brigades de Vigilance* were a group of teenagers and young adults full of hope and patriotic fervor who had organized neighborhood watches to protect their homes and families from the *zenglendos,* those armed gangster remnants of the Duvalier militia or Tonton Macoute. "The orders are clear," Lieutenant Colonel Franklin insisted. "Anyone that stands in the way of the success of the operation must be eliminated."

"Yes sir!" the sheepish officers responded. They added names like Raymond Exulien, Pierre Latortue, Guy Mompremier and Ronald Benjamin St. Fort, aka Ben-X. It was believed that Ben-X was the main leader of the youth movement and the labor unions. They were to dispatch a squad to Fontamara immediately. Captain Marcelus would be in charge of the operation. Ronald St. Fort must not excape under any circumstances. It was later learned through various sources that close to 40,000,000 dollars was raised to finance and support the day's events.

The army officers were no longer accountable to the country they had sworn on their honor to serve and defend, but to a group of international drug dealers who funded them. It would be very hard not to deliver the goods after collecting such large sums of money. The old rules of the game were still at play. "L'argent est le nerf de toutes les choses."[6]

"Ou manage lajan Chada, fok ou paye Chada." ("You eat Chada's money, you must pay Chada back.")

Some of the officers present at the meeting did not have much to say; however, they felt that it was imperative that they be there. They did not want their absences to be misinterpreted as a lack of approval. Fearing the consequences, they lacked the courage to protest. By their silence, they had become accomplices to the crime in progress. The meeting ended with self-congratulatory accolades. The men toasted with imported champagne from France, graciously offered by store owners and businessmen of downtown Port-au-Prince. After having placed death sentences on thousands and thousands of people, these protectors of the state were congratulating themselves as if they had saved the country from an abyss that only they had the power and wisdom to foresee.

Notes

1. "Mothers, tighten your belts." (Prepare yourselves.)
2. Gangsters.
3. Voodoo priest.
4. Bums.
5. Enlisted men.
6. "Money is the nerve of everything."

4

5:30 P.M.: Midtown Port-au-Prince, Avenue Caraibes

The lieutenant colonel knew what he was talking about. Broadcasts were suddenly interrupted in the middle of sentences as scores of bullets, grenades, and firebombs were tossed through the windows of several radio stations. Radio Caraibes was hit particularly hard since the host, Joseph Dorvil, was well known for his direct attacks on the army generals and high-ranking officers. He often characterized them as prostitutes who were ready to sell the country for a part of the illicit drug market. He went as far as to say that he did not understand why such crooks were still walking around untouched in a nation that was trying to establish itself as a place where law and order could prevail. It was as if the rogue army were waiting for the first opportunity to make him pay. He was pulled out of his broadcasting booth and beaten to the point of disfigurement. He was mutilated, his tongue pulled out and cut off. After that he was shot thirty-seven times at close range. The torturers had been so busy killing Joseph Dorvil that they had forgotten to turn off the microphone. Had it been planned this way for some special effect on a now prostrate Haitian population, or was it yet another sign of arrogance? For there would be no indictments, no arrests, no investigation, and no trial for this hideous crime. Joseph Dorvil's body was dragged into the middle of the street in full view of everyone and abandoned to hungry dogs. No words were spoken. No words were needed. The silent message was loud and clear. If you badmouth the Armed Forces and their allies, the same fate awaits you.

Death and intimidation were the order of the day. The world would not forget what happened in Port-au-Prince. It did not matter that the news had been sanitized so as not to upset the stomach of the civilized world, as it ate its dinner while watching the evening news. Nor did it matter that the reporters from the major news agencies insisted on interviewing only white collar workers and residents of the glitzy mansions of Petionville who munched on imported crackers and *foie gras.* The views presented by the major media were slanted toward the rich Haitians, the very financiers of the coup. The number of victims remained at a fixed 3,000 in spite of ample evidence that large-scale massacres were still in progress. The reporters, from their vantage point, only saw the exuberant faces of outspoken lawyers extolling the courage of a valiant army, as if the soldiers had just returned from a war. The truth was there for everyone to see. What mattered was that Haitian society was sinking rapidly into the Dark Ages of barbarism. Every bit of humanity was being sapped out of the nation. It was extremely and exquisitely painful for members of the Haitian diaspora to accept any ties, any kinship to the perpetrators of this horrible crime against humanity. Each expatriate felt a bit of survivor's guilt that day. In the comfort of their mortgaged homes and their apartments, they watched the news of a land that all of a sudden seemed so foreign. What happened to that idyllic country that they had dreamed about for months after they left? What happened to honor and respect, those two little words that had characterized anything Haitian? Maybe it was time that the whole country acknowledge this pain.

Cry Oh Haiti, Cry

Cry oh Haiti, Cry!
Let the tears roll down your tired cheeks.
You have been dealt 101 blows, and yet like a battered woman you have kept your silence.
Cry oh Haiti, Cry!
And in testimony of the suffering you have been through, you have your scorched hills, your malnourished orphans, your dilapidated cities.
Cry oh Haiti, Cry!
All over your body, knots and bruises tell of the abuse and betrayal inflicted on you by your own children.
Cry oh Haiti, Cry!
Looking at your anguish I often wonder
Didn't you many years ago shock the world by breaking the heavy shackles off your sore ankles?
Cry oh Haiti, Cry!
Like Judas, your own children have sold you over and over for thirty dinars and the promise of power.
They have allied themselves with your enemies to keep you in bondage.
Cry oh Haiti, Cry!
So many have claimed to be your friend,
But so few have come to your rescue.
Cry oh Haiti, Cry!
And after you have run out of tears, wash your breast and curse forever those who have mistreated you.
Let your children who have brought shame and abomination on your name be always on the run.

6:00 P.M.: News Bulletin
Distribution: Television Nationale and All Operating Radio Stations
Message to the Nation from Brigadier General Tobias, Commander a.i.

"Peuple Haitien (my fellow Haitians): Today, conscious of its historical mission and its duties vis-à-vis the nation to protect the Constitution and safeguard lives and properties, the Armed Forces of Haiti has deposed Jean Bernard Alexandre of his duty as president of Haiti. The former president has betrayed your trust, and had been preparing to train and arm a militia in violation of the Constitution of 1987, as others have done in the past. Furthermore, he has been exploiting the misery of our less fortunate brothers by inciting them to covet the property of our businessmen and women. He has divided our nation and has failed in his mission to be the president of all Haitians. It has also been discovered that he is mentally deranged and is receiving psychiatric treatment. He has chosen voluntarily to leave the country temporarily until the situation is clarified. The Armed Forces of Haiti, in a courageous act of selflessness, has taken steps to save the democracy for which we all long. This heroic act will be judged by history as an act of 'correction democratique' [sic]. I hope that the parliament will convene soon to acknowledge the presidential vacancy and take appropriate actions to run the business of the state. *Les affaires du pays doivent continuer.*[1] I ask everyone to remain calm and to avoid the usual *provocateurs* and *fauteurs de trouble* (troublemakers) who will attempt to exploit the situation for their own personal gain. The police departments in all the cities will take appropriate measures to ensure the safety of your families. A curfew of seven in the evening will be observed throughout the country. All permits for public gatherings are hereby suspended. Once again, I advise you to stay home and stay calm. God bless you!"

These words were the trademark of the Duvalierists. They just loved those words. Why did they feel obligated to always bring God into their sordid affairs? Who knows? The speech had been delivered very hastily, as if the commander had been forced to deliver the demagogic spiel that neither he, his wife, his son, nor the Haitian people believed. The entire speech was hypocritical. What it did not say was that under the Constitution, it was illegal for the army to seize power, or to call the parliament in national assembly. Once again, the Constitution, voted for and approved by the vast majority of the Haitian people in a rare display of patriotic fervor, was stepped on, as were all the ones before it. The force of the gun and the bayonet once again prevailed.

Was the brigadier general being advised by his PR consultant, or was he the mere executor of a plot conceived out of the headquarters in Virginia? How could a man with a wimpy reputation act so audaciously? Would he have chosen to commit such an act if he did not have some kind of guarantee that he would succeed? Did he feel that he was out of the reach of an angry populace that would certainly not have hesitated to wrap a gasoline filled tire around his neck? Was his crime any different from that of the black members of apartheid South Africa who collaborated with the white masters to oppress the blacks and force them into submission? It was as if Brigadier General Tobias had just made a pact with the devil. The fate of the country and the events that would ensue within the beleaguered island nation would trace their roots to this treacherous act. Would General Tobias have the courage one day to take responsibility for causing the degradation of the country with this dishonorable act? Very unlikely. It would take an inordinate amount of courage, and Brigadier General Tobias had just proven that he was not capable of such valor. He had just betrayed a whole nation. He had strangled a whole people, taking the last breath out of them. A whole nation was moribund; the dream of a free nation living under democratic rule was quickly dying. The previous twenty-five years of popular struggle in Haiti were being erased with a magic wand. Had the Haitians once again been fooled into believing that the very nations that had spent infinite resources and energy to keep them in a state of dependence and virtual servitude would want them to have a taste of democracy *a la Americaine?* How could it have been possible to imagine such a possibility in a country with a literacy rate no higher than 15 percent? How is it possible to believe that an election could magically erase a tradition of mismanagement and pillaging of the resources of the state? Did the proponents of the election really believe it, or had they once again attempted to deceive a nation of dupes? Or was it that the Haitian people were so hungry for democracy that they were ready to accept anything? Electing a leader without the democratic institutions that he needs to govern is a sham. Some elements of the Haitian society whose only experiences with parliament had been learned from Duvalier's handpicked *deputés j'approuve*[2] were about to be transformed into lawmakers and advocates of a democratic society. Where were the members of the Judiciary? Who was going to render justice? Were the crimes of the thirty-year regime going to go unpunished? Electing a leader without the economical means to provide his people with the basic necessities of life is a joke. A leader may claim to be the messiah in order to rally the people behind him so that he may be elected. However, once elected, he had better become a baker who is able to bake a lot of bread, or at least surround himself with real bakers who can make loaves of bread by the thousands. Hopefully he'll not start to believe that he is a real messiah capable of multiplying bread and fish to feed his hungry people. Feeding 6,500,000 people with five loaves of bread and two fish would be a real *tour de force* even in biblical times.[3] At that point he incurs the risk of being put to death by his own people, as was the Messiah. Then, the "messiah" has to resort to gimmicks and tricks to appease the clamors of a population whose demands for justice, food, and participation in the affairs of the state have remained unheeded. How long can one expect the masses to live on empty words? How long can the masses live on vain promises before they become disenchanted, disillusioned with the democràtic process a *la Americaine?* In the spiritual sense, it is a truism that "People need more than bread for their life; they must feed on every word of God." (Matthew 4:4). In the temporal sense, the fact that the masses cannot live on words alone is even truer. As the French adage goes, "Ventre affame n' a pas d'oreilles." (A hungry stomach has no ears.) As far as the masses are concerned, both the question and the answer of Emmanuel-Joseph Sieyes in the day preceding the French Revolution remain the same. What does the Third Estate (masses) want? To be something in it (the political order). In a true democracy, no prophet is above the prophecy. No leader is above the political platform articulated by the majority of the people, the masses. A leader is a standard bearer, a message carrier. The more such a leader symbolizes the struggle of the people, the more electable he or she might be, in a direct suffrage (one person, one vote) election. The elected person might not necessarily be the most effective leader, but he is expected to be a talent gatherer. Electing a leader without the political will and the backbone to create a new society and to put to justice anyone who violates the rules of the nation is a farce. The struggle of the people must go beyond the messiah of the time. The Chinese Revolution has been allowed to perpetuate and survive because it has gone beyond the cult of Mao Zedong, the father of the revolution. In a country with so many unfulfilled needs, one cannot govern without a backbone. In the age of satellite television transmission, the advantages of charisma and eloquence are not to be minimized, but it is not—repeat, it is not—enough. There is always the danger that the enemy of your cause can use the leader's charisma and speaking abilities to caricature him and portray him as an empty drum that resonates well. The Haitian people will sing and dance to the rhythm. After all, Haitians are madly in love with drums. They will take to the streets in no time for you, especially when the orator understands their demands and is able to articulate them well. Whenever such a charismatic leader is allowed to play the electoral game, he will beat all the other candidates combined. One man. One vote. *"Se pa lajan. Non."* (It is not money.) What happens after the election? *Epi? Epi anyin!* (And then? Then, nothing!) Nothing will happen when your enemy holds the purse strings and you inevitably have to go back to him to beg for a quarter to feed your people. Maybe the Haitian people do not expect to be able to eat every day. Their proverbial patience will buy any leader some time. What about justice? It is extremely doubtful that they will want to wait for justice.

In the 1990s, the Haitian people needed just about everything, but what they yearned for the most was a modicum of justice. Everyone seemed to have missed the boat on that one. Was the island nation condemned to be a powder keg ready to explode because its demands for justice had been ignored? Members of the masses who had crossed over and cooperated with the enemy because they could not bear hunger were put to the most inhumane and atrocious deaths. They were given *Pe Lebrun*[4] while the true enemies of the people were allowed to go free, untouched. We are reminded again of Jean de La Fontaine's fable "The Plague-Stricken Animals." In that fable, the lowliest of all the animals, the donkey, was made to pay, while the lions and the sly fox were allowed to get away. Some of the Haitian traitors had no shame hiding under the mantle of the Catholic prelates. The masses are never afraid of sacrifices. They will forgive a leader for making tough decisions, no matter how seemingly cruel, no matter how costly, as long as those decisions are fair. The masses will not forgive a leader for indecisiveness, favoritism, or betrayal of the very issues upon which they chose the leader in the first place. The way that the masses see it, if anyone should be favored it should be them. They are ready to kill for their leader or be killed. The latter eventuality is by far the most common. For every dispute between political factions, the masses pay the price in blood. Their blood. It doesn't matter who is fighting. In pagan times, as the leaders feasted on meat and wine in preparation for war, animals were offered in sacrifice to the gods. In today's Haitian society, what do the leaders do? They have themselves a carnage in the city slums. The only difference is that centuries of civilizations have left their imprint upon the world. For better or worse, the Haitian society has resisted technological advances or it has been kept away from them. Haitians have adopted the corruption and the violence, but not the technology and the explosion of information exchanges that have occurred. There is a revolution going on with communication and information, yet Haiti is still not part of it.

The suffrage of 1990 was extremely important from a historical perspective. For the first time, the masses were electing a leader of their choice in defiance of the international kingmakers, coup makers, wheelers, and dealers. However, it would seem that the relevance of the suffrage from a purely socioeconomic perspective was compromised from the start by the lack of the necessary prerequisites. It did not matter who was elected. It did not matter how popular the chosen one was. The elected one was doomed from the get-go.

Notes

1. "The affairs of the country must continue."
2. Yes-men.
3. Matthew 14:18: Jesus fed 5,000 people with five loaves of bread and two fish.
4. Necklacing; setting a tire on fire and putting it around a person's neck.

5

Any Home, Any City, Haiti

6:15 P.M.

There is complete consternation on the face of every single Haitian. In every home, on every face, uncontrollable tears. How can this be happening? Didn't we make it clear at the polls that we did not want those scums anymore? Didn't we elect Jean Bernard Alexandre by a landslide? We made sure that the margin of victory was wide enough. We did not want anyone to question the results and say, "You know, the results are too close to call." Especially after the American bigwigs wanted our candidate to sign a document accepting his rival as the victor well before the votes were even cast. Can you imagine the audacity of these people?

These were the questions in the minds of most Haitians. They had played the electoral game. The army and its foreign masters did not like the outcome so they were nullifying it. Will the masses ever show so much enthusiasm again and vote in such large numbers? Maybe that is exactly what the coup makers wanted. It is much easier to manipulate the results of an election when participation is low. As long as the big players are willing to play the democratic game in Haiti, and as long as the masses are allowed to be counted as one person, one vote, the Jean Bernard Alexandres of Haiti will always win. With the demographic explosion that is taking place, the masses will always remain a voting block that cannot be ignored. Unless, of course, it is the intent of the internal community to let population control take place in Haiti via massacres, natural disasters, unexplained fires in the slums, deaths at sea during a massive exodus, famine, disease, AIDS epidemics, and so forth.

Not everyone in the Haitian masses thought Jean Bernard Alexandre was blameless. He behaved more like a bishop than a president. He was much too naive to believe that he could convince his enemies to cooperate with him in rescuing the country. He did not seem to have a vision about how Haiti should be governed. If he did, he did not tap enough of the large brain trust that Haiti possesses inside and outside the country to carry out his plans. He overestimated his ability to keep the rogue and corrupt Haitian Army in check. He should have armed and trained his backers. In American culture, this is called Monday morning quarterbacking.

Jean Bernard Alexandre was too much a priest, too much of a nice guy. All of this nonsense about a marriage with the army . . . if only the church had not intervened to stop the *déchoukage*,[1] none of these drug dealers would be here today to betray the trust of the people. He had all of these Tonton Macoutes in his entourage. But he should have armed the people. After the coup, everyone both inside and outside of Haiti was expecting some kind of an armed response, a popular uprising, as part of a grand contingency plan. There were strong indications that the Duvalierists had not given up hope of re-seizing power. While the party in power pontificated, still feeling inebriated from its unprecedented and resounding victory at the polls, the opposition had rekindled and systematized its alliance with drug and arms traffickers. It had found natural allies in the bourgeoisie of Haiti, nostalgic for the huge 600-dollar-a-person parties under the Duvalier regime. No armed response came, no tit for tat . . . because maybe there was no plan. Or perhaps, contrary to what was widely reported about his ability to instigate violence, Jean Bernard Alexandre *was* a genuine apostle of non-violence.

There were a lot of disappointed people in the Haitian diaspora. They believed that a violent attack on the defenseless Haitian people warranted an armed response. There was a war going on. The problem was that one side seemed to have the weaponry, while the other side suffered all the casualties. There was a lot of anger and disbelief, but the prevailing mood was more one of immense disappointment and disgust. The Haitians were in a lot of pain. Only a few months before, they had gone through a very elaborate process of symbolic mourning. Many people had made the pilgrimage to Fort Dimanche: the dungeon where many lives had been cut down in the prime of their youth. They had visited the cells, had read the messages inscribed on the decrepit walls describing the despair of inmates gone mad, with the realization that they would never see freedom again. Banners had been put up. Vows had been taken. Never again! Never again! Alas! Words were not enough. Words are never enough. It all seemed so remote now. The power of money and the gun had once again prevailed over emotions. While the adepts of change had been congratulating themselves over their unprecedented victory at the polls, the forces of darkness were licking their wounds and making alliances with drug dealers and other imperialist interests. The events were certainly tragic, very tragic, but for some reason the whole scene seemed like a giant puppet show with the strings under the hairy finger of a gigantic monster. At each jerk of the string, real people were dying. It had happened over and over in Haitian history.

8:00 P.M.: Fontamara, a Southern Suburb of Port-au-Prince

As ordered, a squad of uniformed soldiers and *attachés* arrived in the Fontamara neighborhood, Uzis and machine guns in hand. They canvassed the neighborhood and started to empty their weapons. On cue, the front doors to various homes flew into pieces. Sleeping children were suddenly awakened to cling one last time to their dying parents or brothers and sisters. There were streams of blood all over. In the house at the end of the street, there were seven dead and one wounded. Scratch that! No one is supposed to know about the wounded. The squad must have had very good information. How could they possibly have known the whereabouts of Ronald St. Fort, who had been maintaining a low profile, at the residence of his adoptive parents, the Lespinasse family? A special armoire with the bottom opening into a deep excavation big enough to hide a person had been built for a day like this. It is probably what saved Ronald's life. Everything happened in less than fifteen minutes. A series of shots from a machine gun. People who could not yet spell the word *Constitution* were losing their last breaths in the name of that very Constitution. From his hiding point, Ronald could hear the muffled voices of the gunmen.

"Let's go! I think this one is already dead!" said a baritone voice.

"Why are you in such a hurry? We have not found St. Fort, the terrorist, yet."

"Boss Joe, remember that I am the commander of this operation. I give the orders."

"Yes, Captain Marcelus! *A vos ordres, mon capitaine!*"[2] Boss Joe continued, "I thought that Lieutenant Colonel Franklin wanted the terrorist's tongue or finger. I will not take any blame for it later."

Ben-X was thinking that even in crime, the partners could not agree on how far they would go with their hideous crime. His heart was racing. He could neither breathe too hard nor sneeze. As his mother and sisters were being tortured, he contemplated leaving his hiding place and giving himself up. But then he thought, "What difference would it make?" It would be like granting his enemy total victory. He, too, would probably be tortured and killed, leaving his struggle unfinished. It would be a total failure. Surrendering would have amounted to suicide. He would just be another victim, just another casualty of a war against the Haitian population, thought Ronald. What on earth could push a human being to lose his humanity and become so barbaric? What crime could Ben-X or his family have committed to deserve such a fate? Ginette was only six years old. Why did she deserve to die? For money? How much money? For the wish to dominate others and stake one's claim on a country? For the wish to make a country one's fiefdom? For what reasons? To deal weapons and drugs? At least during the Cold War era one fought and killed for an ideology that would lead to a better world for all. True or false, it seemed a much more noble, much more magnanimous and altruistic reason. What have the leaders and the trend setters done to the innocence of the world? Wasn't the world promised that there would be no more holocausts? Six million lives in Europe—6,000 lives in the small Haitian Republic. What difference does it make? Crimes against humanity then, crimes against humanity now.

Ronald waited another hour before he ventured out of his hiding place. Staying any longer carried serious risks. The killers were likely to come back to the scene. They always came back, just like vultures always return to their prey until it is reduced to the very carcass. There were no words to describe the scene that Ronald saw when he opened the doors of that tall oak armoire. He was full of rage. Tears flowed from his eyes like a torrent. He felt like screaming but no sounds came out. Maybe it was better that he did not cry out. He did not know where the killers were. Had they left for good or were they still roaming around looking for loot? His six-year-old sister, Ginette, was holding desperately to the arms of her mother, whose nightgown was pulled over her head, her genitalia exposed. "What have those butchers done to my mother?" Ronald demanded. Caroline and Joceline, ages sixteen and seventeen, lay dead, their long and beautiful black hair hanging off their shoulders. What crimes had they committed to have their lives put to such a screeching halt? There they were, lifeless. The expression on their faces was one of extreme surprise. They had been surprised by death just as they were getting ready to begin living. Joceline had been preparing for her final year in secondary school. She had always been at the top of her class and had her mind set on medical school. Caroline had wanted to be an architect and had just won first prize in a Caribbean drawing contest. All their plans were prematurely and suddenly aborted. Ben-X was numb.

Closing the eyes of his sister, he made a solemn vow: "I promise you, Caroline, Joceline, Ginette, and Mom Angeline, I will make them pay for this . . . I swear." He then kissed each of them on the forehead and disappeared into the night. Through all his sorrow, a name kept coming back in his head: Captain Marcelus . . . Captain Marcelus . . . Captain Marcelus. Like a thirty-three rpm record stuck in the middle of a song, the words were repeating themselves over and over. Ben-X would never forget that name for the rest of his life. One day, he would meet this man, face to face. It would be the duel of the century.

Ben-X had adopted a completely different look. He was now wearing a wig, his mustache and beard hastily but closely shaved. His face looked as smooth and clean as that of a nubile woman. It was astonishing how a pair of glasses had changed his appearance. The latest clothing trend was baggy and oversized, which made it relatively easy to disguise himself. Ben-X was wearing a long gray skirt with a light beige top. Nothing flashy—just enough to cover his masculine features. Until further notice, he would be Claudette.

Notes

1. Uprooting.
2. "By your orders, my captain."

6

12:00 P.M. to 12:00 A.M.: Any Town, Haitian Diaspora

From every metropolitan city with a large population of Haitian immigrants: Montreal, New York, Miami, there came the same reaction. All activity had suddenly stopped. Haitians were excused from work. Everyone was glued to CNN or to his or her shortwave radio. Spontaneous gatherings were held in which large signs denouncing the conspiracy among the CIA, the drug dealers, and the Haitian Army were raised. They pointed out the hypocrisy of the American government, which proclaimed its faith in democracy, while stabbing it in the back only hundreds of miles away. The discussions continued well into the night during those first twenty-four hours, as they would for weeks, months, and even years later. Somebody somewhere had decided that democracy was too precious to let the black Haitians taste it for too long. The public relations agents were unleashed very early in the game. Many clubs and families were visited by foreigners flanked with pretty Haitian women describing the misdeeds of the popularly elected president of Haiti. Tracks (leaflets distributed by the army supporters) were distributed. Phony psychiatric reports of President Alexandre were widely distributed. "Jim Crow" from the U.S. Senate demonstrated with great eloquence and a flip chart how the priest president was a psycho, a communist, and likewise.

It was a very somber day in all the Haitian communities abroad. No merengue or compas music played on the radio stations. Only the partisans of the recently defeated candidates could find some reason to rejoice. It was their hope that the cards were about to be reshuffled. Maybe this time they would win more than 3–5 percent of the votes.

Day Two

7:30 A.M.: Ti-Tanyen near Sources Puantes (a Swamp Area Rich in Natural Gas a Few Miles North of Port-au-Prince)

The population awoke in a state of sheer terror. Throughout the night, the characteristic noise of the diesel trucks was heard over and over, together with the bursts of submachine guns. Scores of people had been rounded up from the populous slums of Cite Soleil, Carrefour, and Sans-Fil, and killed. It was reported that hours after the last gunshots were heard, one could distinctly detect the faint sounds of dying people, critically wounded, begging to be put out of their agonizing pain. One woman in her forties, with a large laceration across her abdomen exposing her internal organs, was picked up by a Good Samaritan and rushed to the hospital. She also had several gunshot wounds on her limbs. She had managed to crawl up to the main road, determined to survive to tell the story. For days to come, an unbearable stench from decomposing bodies and the strong smell of sulfur emanating from the ground rich in natural gas would fill the air.

8:00 A.M.: Hôpital de L'Universite D'Etat D'Haiti (State University Hospital of Haiti) Morgue Principale (Main Morgue)

The unit manager had been called out of his bed the previous night. He was under strict orders not to speak to any reporters. No drawers were available in the large refrigerated room. Some of the victims might still have been alive when they were transported to the morgue, but it did not matter. They were so badly wounded and disfigured that they had no chance of survival. They would not have wanted to survive. There were teenagers, young adults in their early twenties, babies, and elderly people. They came almost exclusively from the slums around Port-au-Prince. There was not one reported massacre from the affluent neighborhoods of Petionville where the million-dollar mansions were. It was an apocalyptic scene that should have been captured on film. It was another rendition of the umpteenth Haitian holocaust. Not that it would make any difference. Most of the time people saw what they wanted to see.

In the room there was a strong smell of fresh blood mixed with human waste. There were just too many corpses and too little air. Which one of these victims could ever have imagined that he or she would have suffered such a terrible and tragic end? Which of these young men and women could ever have imagined that the democracy that they had fought for would have come to this? They had had a flicker of hope. Alas! It had lasted as long as the blinking of an eye. A few hours, a few days and it had all come to a brutal halt. Along with their lives, this group of young victims had been robbed of their dreams. In this room, how many doctors? How many lawyers? How many inventors? How many poets and artists? Had those butchers in uniforms any idea that killing this young generation was like draining all the sap out of a dying tree? It seemed like the whole country was lying there on that floor, lifeless. Every square inch was occupied. There must have been at least 1,200 bodies littering the red-stained floor. Someone had seen some humor in all of this and had put up a handwritten sign:

No Vacancies.

What a sinister sight! Would the souls of all of these people ever find eternal peace, or would they wander forever and haunt the dreams of the coup makers and their supporters every time they closed their eyes? Would the images of these corpses torment them and stay with them every single minute of the rest of their useless lives? Unlikely! Like a cat, the devil seems to have many lives.

8:30 A.M.: Trauma Unit

The interns and residents were having the training of their lives. Every known physician had been called to duty to man this overcrowded unit. There was no gauze, no sterile gloves, no lidocaine, no plasma. Gunshot wounds. Stab wounds. Second-degree burns. Not everyone could be attended to. There was a war going on. Yet only one side has the weapons. How unfair.

Pain. Fear. Despair. Weeping. Suddenly, more commotion: A strange character in civilian clothes and armed to the teeth burst into the treatment room. How had he found out that this poor man was here? He pulled the wounded man off the stretcher. The gunman looked like an enraged animal foaming at the mouth. "You bastard," he uttered, as he shot the wounded man in the chest. The man went into convulsions. He was shaking like a leaf. The *coup de grace* . . . the crazed gunman shot one more time. Right between the eyes. The man's brain splashed all over the wall.

Not even the hospital could be considered a safe zone. Was there any humanity left in the world? Sister Angelique, the nun in charge of nursing, passed out and fell to the ground. She could not stand the sight of such atrocity. Maybe it was better that way. Had she made any sign of protest her life would have been in danger. Sister Angelique was no angel; she was known to be a no-nonsense administrator who could, without flinching, tell doctors, employees, or even police officers where to go. No one got in Sister Angelique's way when it came to her patients. That morning, Sister Angelique was taken by surprise. She was speechless.

10:00 A.M.: Operating Room I

The anesthesiologist is out. Her fate unknown. She was a personal friend of the deposed president. Not that she could be of use. There are no supplies available. There has been a shortage of oxygen for the past three days. The operating room has been working on a skeleton staff. No one feels safe to be there. The news of what happened at the trauma unit has spread like a brush fire. There was a mad gunman on the loose. No, no, no! There was a whole army of madmen on the loose. Listen to the words of an overzealous enrollee, who suddenly found himself with no drill sergeant teaching him discipline: "We do not want Jean Bernard Alexandre. If he comes back, *il sera parfaitement mort*."[1] Youthful braggadocio or plain stupidity from an uneducated, brash, and unrefined enlisted man? The latter is more likely. Would they ever learn? Hadn't they watched Baby Doc being whisked away on a military plane in his Mercedes-Benz, while soldiers such as him were tossed into the awaiting hands of the angry populace? While the high ranking officials boarded chartered planes, the lowly soldiers and militia had been necklaced with burning tires. What irony! The very underclass that would likely benefit from real changes in the socioeconomic system in Haiti was showing its approval of the events in progress

Note

1. "He will be perfectly dead."

7

11:30 A.M.: Palais Legislatif, Boulevard Harry Truman, aka Bicentenaire

For over two hours, members of the legislative body have been trying to convene. Many members from the party supporting the deposed president have not reported to the convocation for a special session. There is no quorum . . . besides, the convocation itself is unconstitutional, because only the president may call for a special session. After hours of squabbling and fiery political speech, a compromise—no, a *coup within a coup*—has taken place. The number of members necessary to meet quorum has been lowered by a self-appointed new president of the Senate, His Honorable Piedoux: a senator from hell. He is a caricature of a man—an egomaniac who loves to hear himself talk. Presidential vacancy is declared and the highest ranking member of the Court of Cassation, Mr. Boisette, is appointed president ad interim. A *de facto* regime is in place. It was reported that when Mr. Boisette learned that he had just been appointed president, his whole demeanor changed. Not only did he start to shake like a leaf; he also refused to take off his suit. "I am the president!" he would say. He stands a mere four feet, eleven inches tall. Not even his high-heel shoes quite give him the appearance of the peacock that he sought.

4:00 P.M.: Lieutenant Colonel Michael Franklin's Residence, Delmas 31, Port-au-Prince

"I have called this meeting," started the colonel, "because I am extremely angry!" He started to pound on his desk. "You have been ordered to bring back Ronald St. Fort dead or alive. My information officer told me that St. Fort was not amongst the victims at that Fontamara home. When I give you an order, I expect you to carry it out. I want that man's tongue on my desk by this time tomorrow. Before you know it, he will be starting subversive activities. Do you want your families to live in fear of *Pe Lebrun* again?"

The colonel was furious. He had the characteristic smell of Rum Barbancourt on his breath. At one point, he pulled his army-issued .45 caliber revolver and was brandishing it in the air, as if he were about to shoot someone. This made Captain Roger and Lieutenant Agenor extremely nervous. They were standing at attention, and did not dare move one muscle. Their faces were covered with sweat. They kept repeating, "Yes sir!" like a broken record.

Colonel Franklin started to call the frightened officers all kinds of names. "How did you become an officer in the Armed Forces if you cannot even apprehend that terrorist, that troublemaker Ronald St. Fort? Do you realize that this man can jeopardize the success of the whole operation? I have nothing more to say. Tomorrow by this time! Do you hear me? Dismissed! Good luck!" The frightened officers clicked the heels of their shoes, gave their superior the military salute, and left the room. "I need a drink," said Captain Roger.

As it turned out, they would need more than a drink. Several squads were sent into all the heavily populated neighborhoods. Innocent people were arrested and brought in for questioning. They were tortured and released. Some of them were not so lucky. How could they possibly tell the officers where Ben-X was if they did not know? Ben-X was like a chameleon. He had mastered the art of disguising himself and blending in with his environment.

Since leaving the residence of his late mother and sisters, he had moved around quite a bit. One never knew under what guise he would show up. He had safe houses and hiding places throughout the metropolitan area. When he left Fontamara, he had taken on the appearance of a casually dressed woman. He was not overdressed—just enough in order not to attract attention. Presently he was one of many homeless men and women who had abandoned their usual spots to be on the grounds of the hospital. The good nun, Sister Angelica, would not disturb them. What better hiding spot than less than two miles from the Army Headquarters, right under the enemy's nose? His latest hideout offered the advantage of providing Ben-X with a steady flow of information. As the only major public hospital in the whole metropolitan area, l'*Hôpital de L'Université* was a giant clearinghouse where bits of information filtered through. One could easily eavesdrop on discussions about information given to the medical staff in confidence by military officials. Ben-X could monitor the constant flow of bodies being transported to the mortuary after the *attachés* returned from their rampages. The neighborhoods in which the deposed president was popular were hit especially hard. Undisturbed, from his observation post, Ben-X could plan his future moves. He was not without experience in the area of resistance and civil disobedience. He had infiltrated the *braceros*[1] in the *bateys*[2] of the Dominican Republic to organize and help them obtain more humane treatment from the *dueños*[3] of the sugar plantations. He had even spent a few months in Havana, Cuba, where he had received some military training and special courses in the art of surviving in a hostile and repressive environment. This training was being put to good use now.

Ben-X, from the time he was adopted by the

Lespinasses, had felt compelled to prepare himself for the future of his country. Having lived under Duvalier's dictatorship, he had witnessed firsthand what the combination of drugs, corruption, and depravation could do to a country. If Haiti stood any chance at all of escaping complete annihilation, there needed to be a complete departure from the tradition of exploiting the resources of the land for the benefit of a few. Haiti would need to change from an oligarchy to a true democracy—a system based on the informed participation of an enlightened people. There could not be democracy without education of the people.

Ben-X dreamed of becoming a Black Che Guevara. Seeking refuge into a fantasyland was a healthy thing to do and was quite helpful as Ben-X tried to cope with the predicament in which he found himself. He had to exert extreme care and discipline. The less he said, the easier it would be to escape detection. Not only did he need to change his physical appearance, but he also needed to keep his comments on the political situation to himself. He remembered a movie depicting Nazi Germany in which an American soldier was detected by a Gestapo agent when he fell for the Nazi's trick and started to whistle "Yankee Doodle." Likewise, speaking as a well-read intellectual while living among the homeless people would be a dead giveaway. Ben-X needed to show no discomfort in going days without bathing or changing his clothes. He also needed to beg for leftover food like those around him. Ben-X was a natural.

Notes

1. Sugarcane farm workers.
2. Sugarcane plantations
3. Lord of the plantation.

8

Day Three: Aboard the Submarine Intrepid, Somewhere off the Coast of Haiti

Operation "Extract Wisdom Tooth"

Aboard the submarine, Colonel Winfield was engaged in a very hushed discussion with a group of Navy SEAL officers. There were about fifteen of them. They had been summoned from all over the Southeastern United States for this delicate mission. All it took was a beep. They all had made it to their pickup point in Fort Bragg, North Carolina, in less than three hours. Officer Sutherland had to rush out of the hospital where he was visiting with his terminally ill mother. Another officer had to interrupt his monthly weekend visit with his daughter, Sandra. Duty called.

"Our mission is very clear," the colonel started. "We are to extract the identified individuals and bring them back here. Your insertion point is the beach town of Montrouis. You will be met there by one of our agents. The code phrase is *'Quelle belle nuit pour chasser des pintades sauvages!*[1] Our sources indicate that all the subjects have made it safely to the Club Med Resort. The situation is very unstable. Avoid unnecessary use of your high-powered weapons and avoid detection at all cost. If the journalists from the *Washington Post* get a hold of this, the guy from Kennebunkport will have my head. He can kiss his reelection good-bye if this gets out. The conflict in Haiti is not our conflict. Avoid engaging the military at all cost. Remember, your mission is not to beat up these rascals. You have studied the files. They include pictures of everyone to be rescued. I do not want any screwups. Is that clear? Are there any questions?"

The group seemed ready. Most members had been on much more difficult missions than this one, which sounded like a routine search and rescue operation. They had seen action off the coast of Somalia, or more recently in Bosnia where they had to search and rescue downed pilots. The Navy SEAL officers had very sophisticated equipment. Their position on the ground was known at all times through a network of satellites orbiting around the globe. Every move they made was carefully recorded both with handheld cameras and hand-free microphones. The material from each mission would be carefully reviewed for continuous training. The commander would not tolerate any mistakes. There was no mission too far or too difficult for this group, which was commonly referred to as the "invisible unit." They could descend on a place halfway around the globe, strike their enemy like lightning, and get out before the enemy could figure out what had hit them.

The team got off the submarine and boarded a special engine-powered inflatable boat. They were assembled and became fully operational in less than three minutes. They were specially equipped with missile launchers and lamps that could light up a whole stadium. A total of seven craft were ready. Each one was only lightly loaded, as they expected human cargo on their return trips. Operation "Extract Wisdom Tooth" was well under way. In less than ten minutes, the unit was on land. A high-powered gun with scope manned by a sharpshooter was mounted on a small hill to wipe out any hostile fire coming from the main road. The insertion had been planned to avoid army patrols that made rounds once every three hours. Ironically, the real threat to the unit was not from the regular Haitian Army, but from the "*attachés*" who were undisciplined, overzealous, and, therefore, unpredictable. The elite group was ready for any event. They could not afford to leave any casualties behind if they were to keep the operation as secret as possible. "Engage only when absolutely necessary," they all remembered the colonel say.

The contact person came in the form of a young woman disguised as a fruit merchant. She spoke perfect English with a French accent. The leader of the group said the password. They were cleared to proceed. There was only one encounter as the elite force moved swiftly and took control of the perimeter of the main building. The poor man was quickly incapacitated with a single blow to his carotid area. He died instantaneously. His death probably would not be noticed in a country in which people were dying at an extremely high rate. Everyone inside the hotel had been instructed to gather in the basement with only essential items. There they were met by a CIA operative who had helped every member of this VIP group, which consisted of Jean Bernard Alexandre's cabinet members, high-ranking officers who were too close to the president to feel safe amongst the military, and a couple of CIA members whose missions had expired.

It was difficult to believe that this was the same group of people who, less than a month ago, had been running the affairs of the state. They look tired, scared, and hungry. They had not slept for days, since they had to keep moving from one hiding place to the next. Anyone who would shelter these wanted individuals took a tremendous risk and would certainly face immediate death. Well, they were now under the protectorate of the mighty Armed Forces of the United States of America. No physical harm would come to them, but it is doubtful that they would ever recover from the emotional trauma they had endured.

The rest of the operation went without a hitch, except maybe for a tense moment when the minister of justice, who suffered from hypertension, had succumbed to the high emotional charge of the moment. He was given first aid and the operation went on uninterrupted. VIP status has its privileges. These refugees were about to enter American territorial waters on which would probably be the most expensive trip of their lives. First class, all expenses paid graciously by Uncle Sam and the American taxpayer! Ironically, on that same night, a boat loaded with more than 400 Haitians would capsize off the coast of Cuba.

Note

1. "Beautiful night for wild geese hunting."

9

5:00 P.M.: Lieutenant Colonel Michael Franklin's Residence, Delmas 31, Port-au-Prince

The colonel was enraged. He was so furious that he reassigned Captain Roger and Lieutenant Agenor to desk jobs. He went on rambling as droplets of saliva flew across his desk.

"You will remain in the Police Headquarters and answer the phone; you will attend to the office correspondence, since that is all you can do. You are no officers of the Armed Forces of Haiti. You should be ashamed to wear those insignias. Get out of my face, you imbeciles!" The officers left the room, their heads down, offended and humiliated. If only they could get their hands on the colonel, they would wring his neck. The colonel had taken control over the operation.

"From now on, Ronald St. Fort . . . Ben-X . . . whatever your name is, it is between you and me. I will get you, I swear, if it is the last thing I do," the colonel said to himself. He recruited a group of six enlisted men and six *attachés,* and instructed them to circulate throughout the neighborhoods and spread the news that a reward of 5,000 dollars was being offered for information leading to the arrest of Ronald St. Fort, aka Ben-X. A bulletin was read on the national television that was currently controlled by military personnel. It was also read on the radio. Well, that was a strategic mistake. In a country of citizens who were extremely upset by the events of the preceding days, any opportunity to show their discontent and retaliate against the army was sure to be exploited. The colonel, in his haste, had just handed them such an opportunity on a silver platter. Suddenly the telephone lines at the police stations were flooded with calls. Ben-X had been sighted. He had been seen in the sugar fields of Croix-des-Bouquets. He had been seen traveling peacefully on a bus en route to Carrefour. He was sighted in Aux Cayes, 300 kilometers from Port-au-Prince. He had been seen on the beautiful beaches of Jacmel taking a late swim with a beautiful *marabout* woman, undisturbed by the chaos around him. He was even spotted in a military uniform directing traffic in downtown Port-au-Prince. Ben-X had been seen everywhere!

A series of sabotage incidents followed the supposed sightings. Molotov cocktails were tossed into small police outposts, setting them on fire. Police officers were beat up in remote areas. Soldiers were fed laxatives in local restaurants. Every incident was attributed to Ben-X. The inhabitants of Port-au-Prince were having the time of their lives. Meanwhile, the police chief was going nuts and swore about what he would do when he got a hold of Ben-X. Bold and defiant messages in bright red ink were written on every available wall:

Down with the Army
Long Live Jean Bernard Alexandre
Our Only President
Ben-X

There were tracts urging the people to resist and not give in to despair, for their constitutionally elected president would return. Again signed: Ben-X. Ben-X had gained instant notoriety and had become a household name. He had become a legendary figure who symbolized the anger and the disgust of the Haitian people toward the quagmire created by a greedy and corrupt army. He could smile and thank the population for providing him with the best cover imaginable. With so many Ben-Xs around, how could they find the true one? Will the real Ben-X stand up? Not on your life. Ben-X was enjoying the respite, but knew that it would not be long-lived. It would not take long for his enemies to figure out their mistake and devise a different strategy. Ben-X needed to stay one step ahead of them. He was not totally unfamiliar with the controversy in which he found himself. He was one of the few militants who had expressed quite loudly at times his disenchantment with the strategies that were being used by the party of Jean Bernard Alexandre. He expressed his view that the party in power was becoming too complacent and had not done much to sever itself completely from the *petit bourgeois* who had infiltrated the democratic camp in order to remain in power after the downfall of their former allies, the Duvalierists. Rather than push for a more systematic and all-out campaign of popular education and organization, the party in power was more interested in making their new leader more palatable to Uncle Sam and other developed nations. They figured they would ensure a permanent role for themselves, considering that they were the only ones with a modicum of technical training. When you open your door to one Tonton Macoute, you open yourself to all Tonton Macoutes. That was Ben-X's opinion, anyway. At every cabinet meeting, the president had preached the gospel of no compromise with the other camp. No one had listened. As it turned out, the *petit bourgeois* in government sabotaged every effort to improve the agonizing nation. Their favorite line was, "The Americans will never go for this."

Ben-X was a *carte marquée*[1] from the outset and was hardly surprised that so much effort was being put forth to capture him. Wherever Ben-X went, calamity awaited. The *chefs section*,[2] having been abolished only months ago, came back with a vengeance. They were extorting money from everyone. With all the masses from the capital seeking refuge in the countryside, business was flourishing for the *chefs section*, who made the laws, enforced them, and executed them with the help of a small army of deputies.

The people of Haiti were succumbing rapidly to a reign of terror. The times were comparable to the darkest days of the Duvalier dictatorship. Ben-X was quickly running out of disguises. He had even managed to travel under the guise of a soldier. He had the uniform, the boots, the ID, and even the army-issued .38 caliber revolver. This particular act of audacity scared him and brought to mind the vision of MacArthur saying, "I shall return" as he retreated from the shores of the Philippines. With those thoughts, Ben-X had pretty much decided that he would have to leave the country. Maybe he would make it to Miami and return to Haiti later. Ben-X was brokenhearted, for he felt that his place was among his people, resisting with every breath the terror and infamy that the army had brought upon his country. "There is no shame in retreat if it is what you must do. Do not claim victory just yet, Colonel Franklin; I am not done yet. . . . "

11:00 P.M.: Parcot, Port-au-Prince, Fanmi Se Lavi Orphanage

Over thirty children lived in the Fanmi Se Lavi Orphanage. There were orphans, abandoned children who had been picked up off the streets and given a place that they could call home. They took pride in showing off their talents at sculpture, woodcrafts, painting, and other useful vocational trades. Under the sponsorship of the president, all this group of youngsters ever wanted was to succeed. That night, someone wanted them dead. The light had just been turned off after a short evening prayer. The children were told that the country was going through difficult times, and that they needed to pray and keep faith that the Lord would deliver them. Many children cried that evening because they had known the president personally. They remembered the president, guitar in hand, as he led them in a hearty sing-along.

Signs of trouble came at about eleven o'clock in the evening. There was a strong smell of gasoline and then an explosion. An incendiary grenade had been tossed through the window. The fire spread very quickly. There was a lot of smoke. There was panic. If not for the quick thinking of a group leader, there would have been many deaths that evening. The children were evacuated to a building less than half a block away. Someone called the firefighters. Nobody showed up. The two-story building burned to the ground. What were they going to do? Things had been particularly tough recently. The group could barely afford the three meals that they were usually served. Now they needed to find a place to stay. What could have inspired someone to target these innocent children for such a hideous crime? Someone was thinking ahead, it seemed, and had come to the conclusion that behind every one of these children was the next Jean Bernard Alexandre. How could they not be? They had experienced firsthand what a repressive and unfair society could do to its children. They were all abandoned children. Their parents had been out of the picture for a long time. Placed into domesticity with other families, they were the so-called *restavek*. They lived under a form of childhood slavery, in which children were given menial tasks and subjected to all kinds of physical and even sexual abuse at the hands of teenagers interested in sexual experimentation. These particular children had run away from their households and had been living on the streets until they were picked up by the Fanmi Se Lavi Organization. Why would anyone want to do any more harm to these children? Into what kind of a barbaric society had Haiti been transformed? Why would someone try to emulate that part of human nature that is so savage and shameful that it makes you want to vomit?

Notes

1. Marked card.
2. Army-appointed mob.

Part Two
Escaping the Valley of Death

Bay-Bay peyi mwin, Bay-Bay zanmi mwin
Map di ou o revwa, Pa pou tou tan
Wi fo'm retounin gnou jou lakay mwin
(Bye-Bye my country, Bye-Bye my friends
I bid you farewell, not for ever
Yes I have to return home one day)

—*DPM Kannte,* Jan Mapou, and Kiki Wainwright,
Sosyete Koukouy*

*Used by permission of Frantz "Kiki" Wainwright.

10

Day Thirty-Five

Ben-X had always been a very frugal person. He had suffered as a child and learned to survive on very little. One might even say that he had never really enjoyed his childhood. Over the years, he has learned to save every penny that he could for moments like this. In his backpack, there were a few 100-dollar bills. He folded them and hid them so well in the bag that it would be extremely difficult to find them unless you knew that they were there. He had survived on handouts from charitable organizations and on a network of people who soon had developed their own code of communication. Information was traveling in all directions. By the fourth week after the coup, an underground newspaper was in place and tracts were distributed in most popular areas identifying the "enemies of the people." Many of the youths, having lost all of their friends and family members, had started to jump ship and were becoming informants, as they were promised money, guns, and food. It was becoming extremely risky for Ben-X to find cover. It was time to use his savings and get out.

He made the trip to L'Ile de la Tortue and it did not take him long to find out that boats were leaving the island town at the rate of three or four per week. The question was, which captains could be trusted? A lot of unscrupulous fishermen with absolutely no knowledge of the high seas were capitalizing on the state of desperation that was prevailing in the coastal towns. They swindled people out of their life savings with promises of a safe and easy passage to a land where food was plentiful and where electricity was not rationed. Some of the boats that were touted as seaworthy and ready never left the dock. Sometimes, with the complicity of the local authorities, the trip organizers would disappear to other towns, probably waiting for the next group of candidates willing to take a chance.

The paranoia that had prevailed in the country in the Duvalier era was back. Everyone was afraid of everyone. Any stranger in town could either be a spy for the army, or could be a troublemaker to be turned in for a few dollars or for some special favors. The same masses who had only recently demonstrated their determination by going to the poll were now turning into informants. Ben-X finally decided upon Captain Fombrun. He was able to sell himself as having had experience in navigating small boats. He convinced the captain to take him on in exchange for 900 dollars. The unscrupulous captain would get as much as 1,200 dollars from anyone wanting to secure a place on his small vessel, which could barely hold fifteen people. By the time the preparations were over, the passenger list was close to seventy-seven names long. This expedition had disaster written all over it. However, no one, but no one could convince Haitians about the risk of such a journey, especially when they feared for their lives and had witnessed friends and family members killed in cold blood. At dusk on the hot and steamy Caribbean night, the group embarked on its fateful trip. The name of the small wooden boat was *L'Espoir.*[1] How appropriate! Destination: Miami, United States of America—the land of the free—the land of opportunity.

Disaster seemed to be following Ben-X wherever he

went. There were several false starts as the boat tried to leave the dock. At each attempt, the captain managed to leave a couple of passengers behind. Was the boat overbooked? It seemed obvious that it was. The small vessel could barely move. The boat must have been at sea for only a couple of hours when trouble started. Passengers began to fight for more comfortable positions. Alliances were made with whomever was able to claim real or imaginary leadership. For some reason, the passengers on this sailboat were exhibiting a rather smug optimism. Looking at the size of the boat and the number of passengers, one could realistically say that their chance of making it to their destination was rather slim. Not for this group. Yes, people had succumbed. Everyone on this boat was convinced that because of his or her special relationship with whatever god or *lwa,*[2] he or she would be spared. It did not take long to confirm that deep-rooted belief.

Among the passengers were many high-ranking members of the voodoo religion. One could recognize the face of Paulette, a reputed *mambo*[3] of the region. Rumor had it that she was very close to high-ranking members of the deposed government. She was afraid the military might come after her like they did to many voodoo priests after the downfall of Duvalier. She was carrying many of her sacred objects with her. Paulette's hope was that when she reached Miami, she could establish a little *peristyle*[4] and offer her services to the large Haitian population. Other less famous *hounsis*[5] were also on the boat. The rest of the passengers' beliefs and practices were not as clear, but they would soon become evident. The uncertainty about what lay ahead of them, mixed with the heavy-hearted feeling about what they were leaving behind, was creating a lot of emotional discomfort. Paulette the *mambo* led the group in prayer and song. The passengers invoked Agwe and

Lasiren, the king and queen of the ocean. They sang their hearts out, hoping for a miracle.

Sou lanme ya nap navigue
Agweta woyo gen'w tam ya wè nou

Sou lanme ya nap navigue'oo
Agweta woyo gen'w tam ya wè nou

Yo prem de pye nou, yenchenmede ponyét nou
Yo lagel anba kal
Yo prem de pye nou yenchennen ponyét nou
Yo lagel anba kal batiman

Sou lan mè ya nap navigue
Agweta woyo gen'w tam ya wè nou
—Wawa e Rasin Kanga, Geronimo Records

On the sea, we are navigating Ti lolo
Agwet Awoyo, our day will come and they will take notice
They seize us by the feet, they chain our hands
They throw us in the hold of the ship
—Wawa e Rasin Kanga, Geronimo Records

Some of the passengers were very aloof at first. After all, they had always professed to be Christians and claimed not to believe in the satanic and barbaric voodoo religion. They had their Bibles to prove it, too. When the singing started and several passengers started to fall on the deck, possessed, some of the others began to recite verses from the Bible. For some of the Christians it was their first actual contact with that something inside them that they had always known existed, but had either been forced to ignore or had chosen to ignore. Faced with the intensity of the moment and feeling that they needed all the help they could get, whether it was from Jesus, Erzili, or Agwe, they, too, soon joined in the singing and the invocations. In no time, a small raft was built, upon which offerings of freshly roasted goat meat, rice, sweet potatoes, and *tafia* were placed. For a group embarking on a long and uncertain expedition, it was a very generous offering. Paulette and many others knew that unless their offering was accepted by Agwe and Lasiren, their trip was doomed and they stood no chance of succeeding. As the passengers danced, sang, and spoke in tongues, Ronald St. Fort, aka Ben-X, made his official introduction. He slowly peeled off the sideburns he had glued onto the sides of his face, and removed his mustache and his well arranged goatee. He figured he would not need them for a while and tossed them into the Caribbean Sea. The voodoo ceremony stopped.

Notes

1. Hope.
2. Voodoo god.
3. Voodoo priestess.
4. Voodoo temple.
5. Church assistants.

11

"Who are you?" Captain Fombrun demanded.

"Will you believe me if I tell you?" Ronald responded. From the back of the ship, someone shouted, "I know who he is; I knew it all along. He is Ronald St. Fort—he is Ben-X."

The passengers were mesmerized. "Ben-X!!?" they shouted in unison. The look on the face of Captain Fombrun was more difficult to decipher. It was the look of someone who had been duped. Ayayay! Had he only known what a precious piece of cargo he was carrying, he could have made an easy 5,000 dollars just for turning Ben-X in to the authorities. Besides, Captain Fombrun would have earned the good graces of the military. In his line of business, that was a very valuable connection to have. Ronald knew what the captain was thinking—so did the group of youngsters who suddenly surrounded Ben-X in a spontaneous display of support. "Don't even think about it, Captain!" said the leader of the group, stepping forward as the rest formed a circle around Ben-X. "You will have to kill us first."

What could the captain do, anyway? They were more than eighteen hours into their trip. They were far beyond Haitian territorial waters, but the group that had erected itself into Ben-X's *garde d'honneur* was ready for anything. Ben-X was very moved by this gesture, this act of bravery. After all, it was Captain Fombrun's ship. The life of every member of the group was in the hands of the captain. Ben-X shook the hand of each one of the group of five, as he thanked and embraced them. There was Paul, who was nineteen years old. He had just completed his baccalaureate and was planning on going to agronomy school. Paul was a staunch supporter of Jean Bernard Alexandre. Jean-Robert was seventeen years old and had participated in street demonstrations and acts of civil disobedience from the time he was thirteen. He left the country upon the insistence of his ailing mother. "I probably would die soon after you, should something happen to you," his mother had said. Caroline and Pierre-Michel, both about twenty, completed the group.

"This is very nice!" remarked the captain in an ironic tone of voice. "Now, let's see what happens when I turn you over to the American authorities and identify you as an escaping leftist terrorist."

The captain visibly was not pleased with this new alliance that could become a direct challenge to his authority. But where had he learned how to intimidate people like that? There was one possible explanation. He must have at one time belonged to the Haitian Army or to the Lafontant team of militiamen. The captain was bluffing. He did not have much of a choice. The group, including Ben-X, would have to be extremely careful. Captain Fombrun would seize every opportunity to break them and bring them into complete subordination. The captain obviously had not received any orientation about revolutionary resolve and determination. He was still hoping that one way or another he would assert his authority over the small faction. For now, he decided to play the game of the magnanimous chief.

"Hurray for Ben-X!" he yelled, thumping his heavy worker boots on the wooden deck in a rhythmic fashion.

"Hurray!" responded the excited audience. The clamoring continued.

"Ha peepeep! Ha peepeep!" changed into, "Ben-X! Ben-X! Ben-X!"

There was a new leader on board. It was Ben-X's official coronation. The hero who recently had captured the imaginations of friends and foes alike was aboard. Now Ben-X was under pressure to live up to his reputation. People always develop preformed expectations about their heroes. He was expected to be strong and courageous. He was expected to be selfless and to stand up to injustice. However, in a situation where so many variables were out of our hero's control, Ben-X was walking on thin ice.

The festive mood on the boat was short-lived. It dissipated quickly and changed into a feeling of wariness. As if to confirm the passengers' fears and to remind them that the forces of nature were very much in control of their fate, a sudden gust of wind hit the horizontal part of the mast, nearly breaking it. A shower that lasted less than five minutes but was enough to drench everyone accompanied it. It was going to be a very cold and uncomfortable night. The captain assessed the damage and expressed some hope that it could be repaired. He gave one of his assistants a piece of wire and instructed him to secure the loose piece of wood. Some of the passengers offered to help and formed a human chain, allowing the man to climb up the center part of the mast. He secured the cracked part by making several knots using a pair of pliers. It looked a bit better and would probably last a while, Captain Fombrun concluded after examining the work. The group had every indication that the situation was extremely precarious, but for some reason it did not sink in. There was a prevailing sense that somehow, this group was special—that the gods would make way for their boat and would protect them from detection by Immigration and Customs. Was it denial or a false feeling of invincibility created to compensate for their helplessness in a situation that was beyond their control?

A new sense of solidarity started to develop on the ill-fated ship. Impending disaster has a very strange way of bringing people together. Somehow, in less than a day, the small vessel had become a microcosm of the world the travelers had just left behind. The same chaos had been re-created. There was the captain: authoritarian, dictatorial, relying not on social skills to keep his brethren together, but on brute force and intimidation. Shape up or ship out—and, in this particular case, with deadly consequences. There were the representatives of the different religious denominations, each one feeling self-righteous, as if he or she were holding the one and only key that would open the door to heaven. There were the young people with their strength and intelligence, ready to go to war for whatever they happened to believe in at that moment. There was Ben-X: charismatic, principled, and determined—an indispensable balance to Captain Fombrun's autocratic ways. Finally, there was the large amorphous group of the *sans voix*, the ones who would not dare speak up—the masses who could be used whenever necessary, but who were readily expendable. This was the group that was likely to suffer the brunt of any drastic measures taken for the survival of the small community.

Such a mixture of people in an area less than fifty square feet was bound to become the theater of many contradictory and even paradoxical events. Alliances were made and broken in a matter of hours, depending on where the real or imaginary power shifted. Fights broke out, some because of sexual hormone surges that still occurred in spite of the gravity of the situation, some because close proximity brings out the deepest feelings. Homophobia was rampant. A young man thought an older man was making eyes at him and punched him in the nose. Women were fighting for a little bit more acreage on the overcrowded boat. The frequency of the fights was becoming unmanageable. The safety of the group was threatened. The boat dangerously keeled as groups of people rushed to one side of the boat to avoid flying punches and bottles. Something needed to be done. The captain needed to intervene now and in a dramatic fashion, or else he stood little chance of ever regaining control of the ship. He pulled a whistle from his pocket and blew with all the air that he could garner.

"Quiet!" he shouted. "I want you to listen carefully." The passengers were suddenly silent.

"Lucrece and Raphael, you two started the last fight. Now you must leave the ship. Go ahead and jump!" Lucrece and Raphael, suddenly aware that they were linked by the prospect of their impending demise, were now on the same side. They did not budge. The captain, in a sudden display of gutsiness, moved toward them with a .38 caliber in his hand.

"Get off my boat, now!" he ordered.

His decision was final. Neither the pleas for mercy, nor the cries of despair from the two fighters would reverse the death sentence they had been handed.

No appeal.

No reversal.

No amnesty. The shark-infested waters of the Atlantic would be their final destination. They jumped in the water, hoping against all odds that they would be rescued, rather than killed instantly by the bullets of the crazed captain. Ben-X saw the situation as even more dangerous. He interpreted the captain's decision as a test. Captain Fombrun was trying to provoke Ben-X and his allies. The outcome of such a conflict was uncertain. Should Ben-X prevail, he still would lose because he could not navigate the ship. The captain was an indispensable tyrant, a necessary evil. At least for now, anyway. It was not opportune for Ben-X to engage in a fight at this time. A good warrior chooses his own battles. He picks not just the ones he can win, but the ones that are likely to have an impact on the outcome of the war.

Following the tragic deaths of Lucrece and Raphael, the ambiance became somber and quiet. There was a lull in the fighting but the hostilities remained. There was a cease-fire, maybe out of respect for their departed shipmates who had suddenly become the nicest men on the ship. People in mourning have a tendency to idealize those who are no longer with them. Few agreed with the extreme measures taken by the captain. Does anyone ever agree with a decision taken by those in authority? At least Captain Fombrùn could claim that he had brought calm to the ship. All was calm on the front! Peace was there. Right? Not by a long shot. It was only like the calm within a recently painted sepulcher. Underneath the surface, the passengers were seething with anger, pain, and uneasiness: a situation that could lead to sedition and mutiny. Anarchy was on the horizon. As leaders often do, the captain had misread the situation completely. Since there was no overt protest, he felt that he had at least the tacit approval of his constituency. He was proud of his accomplishment and was beaming with self-confidence. The uneasy sulking persisted for almost three hours. Small groups of passengers formed and everyone was looking at the others, wondering who would have the courage to break the silence first.

12

A young man, probably no older than twenty-two, introduced himself as Paul and boldly initiated a debate. He started with a question that seemed very broad at first, but its analogous nature in regard to the situation at hand was very clear.

"Is it or is it not the responsibility of a leader to ensure the safety of the group by eliminating danger from wherever it might come? What I mean is, should a leader let the whole group perish because of one or two members?"

Caroline, who could not have been more than seventeen, countered with a question of her own. "Are we talking here about an appointed leader, a natural leader, or a *de facto* leader?"

"Why does it matter?" Paul retorted.

"Of course it does," Caroline continued. "When you choose a leader, you entrust him or her with the authority and wisdom to make decisions for you and your fellow citizens. You trust that the leader will be of sound judgment and will make decisions for the common good."

"In an ideal situation you might be right," Paul retorted. "However, most leaders are chosen not on substance or valor, but on charisma and showmanship." Lizette, a young medical student on the run, joined in the debate.

"Choosing a leader is a very difficult task. How can you believe his or her campaign discourse? You know that once elected, leaders rarely keep their promises. Leaders, once established, whether self-appointed or elected, are preoccupied with one thing and one thing only: to remain in power. I don't know if I can trust one person to make decisions that are going to affect my life."

"Are you then suggesting that a country should be ruled only by council?" asked Paul.

"Not necessarily!" Lizette exclaimed. "Councils and parliaments are as good as the people within them. Members of parliament who lack a basic theoretical understanding of the affairs of the state, such as economy, education, health, and law, will only cause more stagnation and chaos."

"A leader should never be chosen," Caroline said, "unless he or she has grassroots support from a party composed of members who are well-educated on the issues. It all starts with a vision based on ideology."

"Do you mean a socialist ideology?" Lizette asked.

"That is exactly what I mean," Caroline quickly responded. "Third-World countries like ours do not have a choice. Unless they unite behind a common vision, a common goal as a nation, they do not stand a chance."

"Ideology! What ideology?" Paul exclaimed. "Look at all these Eastern European countries! Where did their ideology get them? How about Cuba? Wouldn't you say that their revolution has failed?"

Ben-X could not stay out of the debate any longer. He had been to Cuba. He had witnessed firsthand the determination of a people who would not bow to pressure from the United States.

"Tell me about it," Ben-X started. "You cannot say that they have failed. They have one of the lowest rates of illiteracy in the region when compared to other countries of their size and resources. They have at least established their identity as a nation. Have you seen any of their children sell their souls to overthrow the system? Their only problem is that the country has been sabotaged by the United States. They have been asphyxiated, because of the ideology they espouse. That does not make any sense. Ideology has kept the countries with a socialist experience together. Ideology is a catalyst, an enzyme without which there cannot be any real changes, any *metanoia.* The ideological phase is an essential first step for any country that is trying to establish its identity as a nation. Only then is it possible to really address economic development."

"Then how come there are so many negative reports about the state of Cuba's economy?" asked Paul.

"You have to be careful about the sources of those reports," Lizette responded. "Would you expect the United States to say anything good about Cuba after the American policy makers obviously dropped the ball on that one? Their policy toward Cuba has been a complete failure. Had *Blan Meriken* been less shortsighted, Cuba would have been a success and the United States could have claimed some of the credit. A few countries might have followed the Cuban model. The whole area would have been far better off than it is now.

"Now let me ask you this," Lizette continued. "Is Haiti better off than Cuba? You see the American press keeps comparing the standard of living in Cuba to that of the United States. Now, you know that there is no other Caribbean nation with a standard of living comparable to that of the United States. Any elementary school student in Haiti knows that."

"I think that Cuba is far better off than Haiti," Paul admitted. "Look how many billions of dollars are being spent on Haiti. I am still waiting to see some progress."

"Otherwise, countries like ours are condemned to a state of dependency on foreign nations," Caroline intervened.

"Are you telling me that capital is secondary to ideology?" asked Fresnel, who had remained silent until now. "Ideology cannot build roads. Ideology cannot buy equipment for the farm. What are you talking about?"

"Well, Fresnel, if money were all that it took, we would not be here on this boat, would we?" asked Paul. "Do you know how many billions of dollars have been spent in Haiti for the past fifty years? Probably enough to build schools and hospitals in every city of the country and then some." Fresnel did not concede the point.

"The superpowers are not without blame," continued Fresnel. "They have supplied the capital but not without a cost. They cannot resist the temptation to constantly interfere with the formentation of ideology in Third-World countries. This process is essential. Why do they have to be so paranoid, anyway? Look what they did to Cuba. They systematically asphyxiated that country just because of its so-called socialist ideology, and then they turned around, kissed, and made nice with the largest socialist country of them all. Had they let the process take place without interference, Cuba would have probably moved away from stagnation. Eventually, the American government is going to have to spend billions of dollars in Cuba. They will have to make up for wasted time. Go and explain this to the Haitian parliament members. There cannot be any democracy without education of the leaders, themselves."

"What should the Americans do about Cuba?" Carolina asked.

Fresnel and Lizette responded almost in unison, "Just let them be!"

"Open the damn market!" Lizette continued. "Stop the blockade. Maybe there is still time to rescue the Cuban Revolution. The Cubans have a sense of country. A lot of them are educated. They seem readier than most small Third-

World countries for the next phase: the phase of economic development."

"You must be kidding," said Paul. "That will never happen. *Blan Meriken* is too proud to admit that he made a mistake."

Ben-X continued to listen in amazement. It did not matter that the interpretation of the relationship between the Third-World countries and their big neighbors from the North was full of contradictions and sounded rather naive at times. At least these young Haitians were seeing their country as part of a more global world. The oppressive system in Haiti might have stunted their physical growth, but it had not stunted their intellect. He had very ambivalent feelings about what he was hearing. On the one hand, he was happy to note that the calamities and the state of chaos that had prevailed in Haiti had not deterred the younger generations from continuing to think and to develop their own opinions about the political system. On the other hand, it was very sad to note that the intelligentsia of the country was fleeing like cats out of a house on fire. What chance did the country have to ever recover from the stagnation it had been in if all of its young talent were being chased away from the mainland?

The debate continued for hours. Interestingly, the older members of the group did not join in the discussion. Maybe they were too disillusioned, or did not share the wit and political savvy of their younger peers. After a while, it was very difficult to hope that anything would ever change in Haiti. Each new government had come and gone, touting itself as the one that would finally change things. Nada. It seemed as if in the middle of the sea, away from the media and unwanted intruders, this group of extremely bright Haitians was placing the whole Haitian political system on trial. A kind of a trial *in absentia* had just taken place. They had been able to move away from the tragic demise of Lucrece and Raphael and had drawn lessons for everyone. This said and done, the passengers were ready to go through a more emotional grieving process.

13

The outpouring came in the form of a verbal attack. Maybe they were finally feeling their strength as the group had coalesced. They no longer seemed afraid of the taciturn captain. They let him have it. Their voices rose in protest.

"We know we should never have trusted you. What else could we have expected from you? You learned your trade from the *Tonton Macoutes*." They felt free and emboldened by the fact that they had managed to steal Captain Fombrun's gun and throw it overboard. When the captain realized that he no longer had his piece, he became less bullish. The passengers started to sing Manno Charlenajne's song that had recently been banned from radio broadcast:

Le ou fe sa ma pe-ou,
Paske ou se makout.
Ou Konpran ou kap kapon-nin mwin.
Ou rale Uzi-ou la, Mwin relax sou-ou.
Ou rale baton gayak la; Mwin "be cool" sou ou.
I am sorry for you.
Se vre, tonne.
Tonne kraze-m Michele Bennett.
Se nan videyo wa gade pep Ayisyin.
Ou voye papa-ou al achte twa bomb
pou vin-n bonbade la jenes an ayiti ki deklare,
"Dechoukaj la pako fini . . ."*

When you take that posture, I'm supposed to be afraid.

*Used by permission of Joseph Emmanuel Charlemagne.

Because you're a Tonton Macoute, I'm supposed to be intimidated.
You pulled your Uzi. I am all relaxed.
You pulled your baton; I'm cool.
It's true, damn it.
I swear Michele Bennett, I'm sorry for you.
Only on video will you watch the Haitian people.
You sent your father to buy three bombs to shell the Haitian youths because they have declared,
"The uprooting is not over . . ."

As they sang, they danced and made gestures in an impromptu choreography pulled out of their rich repertoire. The teasing went on for some time. Surprisingly, Captain Fombrun kept his cool. That attitude probably saved him from further humiliation. A boat whose captain was no longer in control could spell even more immediate trouble for the travelers. The songs, more daring at first, became more expressive of their grief and sorrow. The celebration took a more somber tone. The whole group started to sing. Even the captain joined in and sang a couple of verses in his rattling voice:

Mwin bral lot bo wa, lakay Papa mwin.
Fatig chemin yan fini pou mwin.
Le ma rive lot bo rivie-ya
Ma jwin Kote pou-m repoze tet mwin.

I'm going on the other side, I'm going to my Father (Lord).
The fatigue of the trip will soon be over.
When I arrive on the other side of the river
I will find a place where to rest my head.

It was like a sudden outpouring of sadness over their departed fellow passengers. Little did they know there would be more opportunity for the *equipage*[1] to display its grief. They sang many popular songs. The lively group joked, laughed, shouted, cried, and prayed. Judging by the loudness of the songs and the enthusiasm displayed by the participants, it would have been easy to believe that there was a party, not a wake, that was going on. They sang gospel songs, voodoo songs, and black spirituals. Simbie, Agwe, and Lasiren must all have been awakened at the bottom of the sea by the melodious voices of this loud group. They chanted the latest Boukman Eksperyans tunes:

Se neg la gue m'ye.
Se baton fe an-ye.
Ki sa yo ka fe mwin?
Kan-no pa fe mwin pe.

I am a warrior.
I am a spear of iron.
What can they do to me?
I am not afraid of cannons.

This group that had been chased by cannons and machine guns finally had an opportunity to vent in a visible attempt at mastery. They voiced their disapproval about what had just happened to their country:

[Bon Die] Pa jan-m bay lod pou moun ka touye moun.
Gnou ban-n mafia ap souse san nou, yo san pitie.
Fok nou pale.
Bon Die pa jan-m bay lod pou moun esplwate moun.

God never gave orders for people to kill people.
Mafiosi are sucking our blood.
We need to speak up.
God never gave orders for people to exploit people.
We need to speak up.

During the last couple of hours, the wind intensity had decreased considerably. The small 100-horsepower engine had been overworked and was showing signs of strain, until it came to a total stop. Captain Fombrun delivered the bad news.

"The boat is not going to make it unless we let off some weight," he said very firmly. The passengers remained unmoved. Captain Fombrun thought perhaps they had not heard him. He repeated himself.

"What I am trying to say is that the boat is not going to go anywhere. We need to take off some weight." No one moved. "I said," he repeated angrily, "we need to get rid of any excess baggage that we might have."

This was going to be extremely difficult. In fact, no one had any excess baggage to speak of. They had consumed almost every bit of provisions they had carried, and some of them were getting hungry and dehydrated. They were in no mood to deal with any bad news. So they chose to ignore the plea of the exasperated captain. Besides, they were not on this boat on account of anyone but their *lwas.* Agwe and Lasiren would get them through. No one would say a word to the captain, but they were all thinking along those lines. Captain Fombrun was getting angrier and angrier, stomping his feet, cursing, and swearing.

"Tonne boule-m, si nou pa commance jete grimas nou yo Kounie-ya, Map Komanse jete nou nan lanme-ya gnoun pa gnoun!" he exclaimed.[2]

The travelers started to collect small items like empty cans, empty plastic bottles and containers, articles of clothing, empty drums, and suitcases. It did not amount to much—probably a mere sixty pounds, if even that. The captain, with the help of some of the men, tried to restart the engine. No success! The boat still would not move. The sense of duty on the shoulders of the captain was increasing with every passing hour. The captain once again had the opportunity to play God. He was the king and had absolute power over the life of these unfortunate travelers. In the back of the boat an old man was drawing on a clay pipe. He must have been over sixty-five years old. His name was Boss Gerard. His face bore the marks of the difficult life he must have lived. Scars and wrinkles competed for the rather small face. The man was small and thinly built. His weight could be estimated at about 110 pounds. He seemed very weak and malnourished. With a very faint voice, he whispered, "I made a mistake coming on this boat. I am a useless old man. I have had my share of joy out of life. I stopped living years ago when my beautiful wife Adeline died. I am greatly saddened by what Haiti Thomas has become. You see, *zanmi mwin,*[3] I am not afraid of death. People who die go to a better place, where *equality* is not an empty word. Everyone is treated the same. Whether you are a king, a president, or a beggar, there is one appointment you cannot miss. When your card is called there is no escaping. My card has been called. I will see you on the other side."

Before anyone could stop him, he jumped overboard. He disappeared into the water and never came back up. At the point where he entered the water, one could see a little twirling motion, the kind that you see when a rock is thrown into a pond. The wise man was gone. Was it an act of heroism or an act of cowardice? This sudden disappearance was just another somber note in a long requiem. There was no knell, no wreath. The turbulent Caribbean Sea had just claimed another soul. Had the wise man found eternal peace, or would his soul wander the sea to torment unwary travelers? It was a tragic end to the life of a man full of wisdom, a man who probably had a lot more to share.

Nothing had been resolved. However, the suicide of the elderly man signaled a turning point in the way that the crazed captain would handle the situation. It had been two days since the start of the trip. Drinking water was scarce. There was water all around, yet people were very thirsty. The group had nowhere to go, no one to turn to. They were resigned to the fact that some of them would meet an untimely death either by exposure or by the force of a captain turned executioner. The group went back to praying, making sure that this time no gods were left out. An old man who claimed that he had been a preacher led the group in reciting verses from David, Psalm 22:

> My God, my God! Why have you forsaken me?
> Why do you remain so distant?
> Why do you ignore my cries for help?
> O Lord, do not stay away!
> You are my strength; come quickly to my aid!

Was God listening to their prayers that day? It did not appear that way. The wind was picking up, but the boat moved sluggishly because it was still too heavy. One could say that the captain did not have a heart and it probably was true, but it took guts to do what he did next. He walked around like a shepherd surveying his cattle, picked six adults—four men and two women—and ordered them in the water. He had decided to offer them in sacrifice for the benefit of the rest. He offered no explanation. Maybe he did not feel he owed one to anybody. It was a jungle out there and in his mind he was the lion king. There was consternation on the small vessel. However, unlike before, the passengers did not remain silent. They went on singing their sorrow. It was more like a long lamentation:

Fey, o sove la vi mwin nan mize mwin ye o.
Pitit mwin malad mwin min-nin'l ka gangan.

Si ou bon gan-gan wa sove lavi mwin
Nan mize mwin ye o.

Leaf, save me out of my misery.
My son is sick and I took him to the houngan.
If he is any good, he'll save me out of my misery.

The purge continued. More passengers were thrown into the shark-infested waters. The boat was moving all right, but at the cost of many lives. It was a colossal fight: the fight of man against the elements, the fight of man against nature. Somewhere in the middle of the ocean, a major taboo had been violated. A cardinal sin had been committed. The principle that dictates that the captain put the life of his passengers ahead of his very own had been pushed aside. It was as if this man, the *maximum leader*, had just declared a state of emergency in his territory and was ruling by decree. So far, all he had decreed was death. The captain's honor was gone. The passengers were caught in the middle of nowhere, ill equipped, exhausted, hungry, and thirsty. They were no match for Mother Nature. They were doomed from the get-go. There were some moments of hope when the group thought they might pull it off. The older members of the group joined in the celebration, contributing folktales. Some of them were as old as the African continent, and some of them had come out of Haiti's more recent past. They were tales that were told over and over by grandparents who had cherished them and saved them like fine jewelry from a treasure chest. They were slightly different each time one heard them, as they were constantly adapted to the necessity of the time. However, the central theme always remained the same.

"Tim, Tim," began the storyteller.

"Bwa sech," the captivated audience would respond. Others would say, "Cric," while the listeners would say, "Crac." It went on and on. They shared stories about Bouki, the buffoon-like character, and Malice, the sly, sleek one who always managed to pull a fast one on Bouki. The analogies between the tales they shared and the situation they faced were, at times, striking. One of the stories almost brought the listeners to tears.

"Once upon a time," an old lady started, "a rat was having a baptism. He decided to have a dance. Who do you think he chose as a DJ? A cat. Well, that was a costly mistake. At around midnight, the cat locked all the doors and ate all the rats, including mother, father, godfather, godmother, and godson. Not even the officiating priest was spared." Of course, the army had been given the task of safeguarding the change of power in Haiti. What had they done? They locked up the country and massacred its children.

There were also less poignant stories, like the one about *Metres Dlo*,[4] which depicted how society should be from a moral standpoint. In the story, the kind nature of a saddened *restavek* girl (servant girl), after having lost the silver spoon of her mistress, is rewarded with a treasure of gold and silver. Likewise, the rudeness, stubbornness, and greed of the mistress' own daughter is punished with "lizards, goblins, demons, and devils that ate the girl up." Perhaps the storyteller was trying to give the passengers some hope that when the chaos back home was finished they would be victorious, while the killers back home would be punished.

It had been over five days since the trip had begun. The signs of animosity and the quarrels that had been so frequent at the beginning had disappeared. The group had grown into a united community in which the passengers were helping and supporting each other. The danger and calamity they had faced had brought the best out of them. They were no longer bothered by the close proximity in which they were living. It did not matter that deteriorating personal hygiene mixed with a lack of sanitation had created a situation beyond description. The young were helping the old. The strong were lending a hand to the sick. Every little bit of feed was shared. Rainwater, collected in empty plastic containers, was passed around for consumption. One person's pain was everyone's concern. Gone was the suspiciousness and struggle for territory that had prevailed at the beginning of the trip. For a few moments, at least, the group was living up to the motto inscribed on their national flag: "L'union fait la force."[5] It did not matter that the self-declared leader of the small community was a taciturn and dictatorial ruler. The will and determination of the people had managed to factor him out. He was one person on one side standing opposite a more cohesive group on the other side. If only the people back in Haiti would develop this same sense of cohesion and community without always blaming their leaders, whether they be self-appointed or elected. Then maybe the leaders, themselves, would feel the popular pressure for more accountability. There were many lessons taught and learned on this small craft, but, alas, it would all be for naught.

Notes

1. Crew.
2. "If you don't start throwing your garbage overboard, I will start throwing you overboard one by one!"
3. My friend.
4. Mother of the waters.
5. "There is strength in unity."

14

There was a storm on the horizon. The captain suddenly seemed very worried. The singing went on, but the sounds were like cries of despair:

Nan Fon Kal Negrie

Nan Fon Kal Negrie
Pa gen neg pase neg
Min-m Koz Min-m destin
Peson pa kab di li pa kon ki les li ye
Nan fon kal Negrie

Adie Bon Die
Lwin lakay, Lwin fanmi
San-l pa vle, li pati
Pou you voyaj manch long
Nan fon kal Negrie

Anba kout fwet Gran Don
Vant sou do, ke nan min, tet leve
Li chante, Li kriye, Li semante set fwa
Pou-l kontinye goumin jouk li jwin libete
Nan fon kal Negrie

Jodi-a zot di nou, nou ginyin libete
Pandan nap soufri anba kod la mize
Nou sanble nou bliye ki seman nou te fe
Non Fon kal Negrie

In the Hold of the Slave-Ship

In the hold of the slave-ship
All for one, one for all
Same fate, same destiny.
No one dares to forget that he is a Negro,
In the hold of the slave-ship.

Alas! Uprooted from his home country,
Away from his family
Unwilling passenger on a long journey
He cries, sings, and laments
In the hold of the slave-ship.

Under the master's whip
Famish, frightened but not vanquished
Each and everyone took the sacred vow
Never to stop fighting until freedom comes,
In the hold of the slave-ship.

Today, told that he is free
While chained by poverty in the world of plenty
He has all but forgotten
The vow that he once took
In the hold of the slave-ship.

The captain was restless. He paced back and forth. He had been through difficult times before, but this time the situation was extremely grave. Not that anyone expected him to have a smile on his face. He was all business. He had made his one feeble attempt to show some feeling when he had sung a few words earlier. The closest he came to smiling occurred when a man in his late forties offered a joke about the ex-commander of the National Palace Guard during the dark years of Papa Doc. It was more of a grin rather than a smile. It lasted only a few seconds.

The captain's eyes were fixed on the patches of nimbus

clouds just ahead of him. He still would not say much. If the worry on his face was an indication of the trouble ahead, the passengers had better say their last prayers. Is there a priest in the house? Last rites are needed. With every minute, the captain was getting more and more restless. For the first time in his life, he was facing the possibility that he might be at the end of his long trip. A trip that, after many turns, had found him on that night at the command of a sinking ship. He was powerless. He could not save his own soul, even if he wanted to abandon ship and run. Run where? It was Captain Fombrun's turn to sing his swan song. It seemed that the curtain was being pulled on the final act of a long play. A play in which Captain Fombrun had had the leading role. He had played the puppet master, pulling the strings. And now the strings had broken. He would leave the world the same way that he had entered it.

Alone.

No trusted friends.

No wife.

No children.

All men have a purpose in life. Captain Fombrun's purpose was to trade, negotiate, and squeeze every dollar out of anyone who happened to cross his path. One would think that he had just heard a weather bulletin calling all ships back to shore. In fact, the captain was so certain about his interpretation of the sky that he did not need any weather broadcast. It is fascinating how this individual who never went to maritime school was able to navigate the ship using the sky as his only compass.

Fombrun had always wanted to be a captain. As a teenager, he spent most of his time in a small fishing boat. He would rather stay on the beach than go to school. He was a beach bum. In the days when Haiti's coastal cities were visited by thousands of tourists, lovers of primitive arts, and thrill seekers, he would linger on the beach for hours looking at the cruise ships, hoping that one day he would navigate one.

Through his connections with the Duvalier regime, he was able to join the small Haitian Marines Unit, even though he did not know how to read and could barely sign his name. His career in the military lasted only sixteen months. His short stay was marred with violent incidents. He had outbursts of rage and repeatedly engaged in fights with the other sailors. He accumulated a collection of reprimands, including one for going AWOL. He went on a training mission to another coastal town, was given a short furlough, and did not report back to his ship on time. There was just too much structure in the military for Captain Fombrun. Sometimes institutions like the Armed Forces seek out such undesirable elements in their midst—they might just be the right people for missions where moral conscience and scruples might get in the way. However, it was too much when Fombrun got into a violent altercation with his commanding officer and threatened to blow his head off. He was out of uniform the next day with a dishonorable discharge. He should have considered himself lucky to be alive, because some officers in the Haitian Armed Forces might have just shot him. He received no court martial. No questions were asked.

For Captain Fombrun, it had not been a complete loss. At least, he had spent some time on the sea as a sailor, and had learned the basics of navigation. It was a pity, because in spite of his lack of academic education, Captain Fombrun had the unique ability to memorize everything he saw. He only needed to see it once to memorize and retrieve it later at the appropriate time. His love for the sea was too strong for him to let his misfortune in the Marines keep him away from boats. He soon was able to own his own thirty-foot boat, and when traveling to the Bahamas and Miami became fashionable, he saw an opportunity to embark on a brand new career. Some might say that he was performing a public service by providing numerous Haitians with their only escape out of a very dangerous and often degrading place. Others might say that he was an unscrupulous character who exploited the misery of people in distress to extort large sums of money from them. He was the person that Haitians love to hate. Sometimes he took up to 1,200 dollars from people, only to bring them to a certain death. He had traveled the strait of the Caribbean for close to ten years now, and often bragged that he knew it like the back of his hand. Well, he needed all his skills and a lot of . . . luck, because a nasty storm was on the horizon. During the past couple of hours, the reality of the upcoming storm had become obvious, even to the most untrained eyes.

The rain came first. It came down so quickly that the old lady who had assumed the function of cook did not have time to put away the pot of cornmeal that she was cooking. What would they eat now? It was pouring very hard. It looked as if the sky had been transformed into a giant sieve that could not hold anything. The passengers could not even hear themselves talking. There was a look of desperation on everyone's face. The situation was critical. It did not look good at all. It had been raining for a good twenty minutes and had not let up. The force of the torrential rain battered the passengers, who had not had a good meal for days now. There was water all over. They could hardly see each other's faces, as the Coleman lantern bounced in all directions at the mercy of the wind. Maybe it was better that way. All the hope that was once reflected on those faces had disappeared. It was an expression that one could only expect in the face of imminent death.

The situation seemed irreversible. The crew had given up directing everyone to try to pump out the water from the ship. How do you get rid of two and a half inches of rain in less than an hour, with no pump, no tools, and, especially, no strength? To make matters worse, a half-meter-wide hole suddenly showed up in the hull of the wooden craft. The captain was all too familiar with the latest discovery. The hole had been patched many times with large shreds of linen material and tar. He had promised himself many times that he would take the craft to dry dock and repair it for good. "Next time," he kept on repeating to himself. Business had been too good for him to take a break.

The wind started to blow with such intensity that people were being thrown on each other with every gust. The sail went out first. It tore to shreds with a loud ripping sound. It did not take long for the mast to follow. It came crashing down, missing a passenger by less than a foot. Panic and pandemonium were the order of the day. Screams, tears, incantations, and prayers were shouted at the same time, creating a cacophony, a final offering of this group in distress. The boat was sinking. People were tossed in the water by the force of the wind. Life jackets would have been helpful. There were none to be found.

The boat was no match for the elements it was facing. Water inside, water outside, water everywhere. *L'Espoir*, the boat that had carried the dream of many men, women, and children, was quickly coming to an end. If this boat could speak, it would tell stories not about hope, as the name indicated, but rather of *des-espoir* (despair). This boat had witnessed deaths by the hundreds. Men and women had been condemned to tragic ends. Their only crime had been to dare to pursue a dream—a dream of freedom and happiness. Was it a crime to do so? If it was a crime, did they deserve to die?

The punishment did not fit the crime. The boat went down very quickly. Everyone was in the water in the middle of nowhere. Some of the passengers gave up very early and drowned right away. Some of them were trying to hold on to any piece of debris they could get their hands on. Some were swimming to nowhere. It would take divine intervention for anyone to survive this disaster. Apparently the gods did not seem to be listening. What had this group done to deserve such a harsh punishment? Had the captain offended the gods when he took it upon himself to send some of the passengers to their deaths? Or had the gods planned it this way all along, with these mortals, these toys, in their powerful and controlling hands? Whatever it was, it seemed quite cruel and calculating. While other countries seemed to be enjoying a renewed sense of prosperity and were embarking on new conquests, the Haitians seemed to still be searching for their souls. Haiti had become a nation of refugees. Even on their own land they seemed out of place. Wherever they went they had been subjected to untold injustice, yet they had displayed indomitable spirit.

For a while, it seemed as if a few of the passengers would survive this disaster. Ben-X and two other men managed to climb on top of some empty drums. They gave each other support, exchanging childhood memories. They repeated the same stories until they became too tired to talk. Their voices were reduced to faint whispers. Ben-X could no longer hear anyone. Eddy signed off first.

"If you ever make it, Ben-X," he said, "I want you to tell my son Karl that I loved him until the very end, and that I have no regrets. I had to make this trip to try to open the door for him. One day maybe I will see him on the other side." These were the very last words that Ben-X heard from any member of that fateful journey. The refugees would never know how close they came to completing their trip. They would never know that if their sailboat had held together a few hours longer, they would have made it to the shores of South Florida. It was the only thing that Ben-X could think of to explain how he found himself still breathing, exhausted on the white sandy beach of Virginia Key. He had no idea where he was, but it seemed that someone with immense power had decided to give him another chance. It seemed that Death had been ordered by the powers that be to hold off calling Ben-X's number.

Wherever he was, Ben-X realized that he needed to stay out of the view of onlookers. He needed to hide until he could figure out where he was. Actually, Ben-X was not alone on that seemingly deserted beach. If he could have taken a long walk, he would have noticed that, spread over a mile-long area, some of his fellow passengers had started to wash up on the white sand of the Miami shore. Their lifeless bodies were disfigured and bloated by excessive consumption of saltwater. Ben-X would have seen Paul, Caroline, and Lizette, even though all of them were barely recognizable. He would have seen those other young men who had stepped forward on the boat in a show of support for him after he had revealed his identity. He would have also seen Captain Fombrun, that enigmatic character who had accumulated a tidy little fortune by selling hope and death at the same time. To everyone else, these individuals would be just another group of black Haitians who lacked the good judgment to avoid a senseless death. To Ben-X, they had human faces, each with a story to tell. Stories of courage and determination, stories full of hopes and dreams that their country would once again be treated with the dignity and respect that it deserved.

Ben-X was hardly alone. In death, his fellow passengers had made it to the shores of a country that probably would have rejected them, had they made it alive. They had not survived and maybe it was better that way. Had they made it alive, they would have been reined in like cattle and taken into captivity to refugee camps like Krome or Guantanamo. The fact that they were escaping the hell of Haiti would have been denied. In death, they had triumphed. Somehow, they had managed to defeat those who stood ready to humiliate them, to declare them expendable aliens. Somehow they could claim victory. Their spirits were free to roam the beaches of sunny Florida, the vacation land where people from all over the world were welcome . . . that is, as long as they had money to spend and were ready to consume the goods that Florida was selling. The lovers and vacationers lying in the sand drinking in the sun so that they might show off their tans had better stay awake. The spirits of the drowned Haitians would haunt their dreams and tickle their feet. They had, in death, come to accompany Ben-X, their hero. Let the knell toll! Let it resonate and wake the conscience of everyone. Heroes have fallen!

Lady Luck was still with Ben-X. There were a couple of hours of darkness left in that breezy Miami night. Ben-X scanned the area. Toward the very end of the beach there was a small beach house. There was no light. Ben-X approached it like a fox. He carefully peeped through the window. He could hardly see inside, but the three-room house seemed unoccupied. Ben-X quickly looked around. One of the windows was open, so he let himself in. It took a little while for his eyes to get used to the darkness. Someone had recently lived in this house. There was a closet with a few pieces of clothing in it. Ben-X helped himself to a pair of blue jeans, a black T-shirt, and a pair of sneakers. They were a bit big, but they would have to do for now. He looked around for some food, but only found some stale leftover biscuits. The place was pretty safe for the time being. It seemed unlikely that someone would show up before late morning.

Ben-X was wrong. By nine o'clock that morning there was a lot of commotion on the beach. He left the area and headed toward the main road. There were ambulances and sirens. There were news trucks. Something big was happening. Little did Ben-X know that thirty-three bodies had washed up on the shores of the beautiful beach. By noon that day, the group that had traveled under the helmsmanship of Captain Fombrun had become famous. The pictures of their decomposing bodies were flashed via satellite halfway around the world. It was a media zoo. Camera crews were all over Virginia Key Beach. As a sign of mourning, all the regular programming was preempted. Only classical music and other appropriate songs were played.

> We no know how we and dem
> A go work this out.
> We no know how we and dem
> A go work it out.
> But someone will have to pay
> For the innocent blood
> That they shed every day. Oh children mark my word
> It's what the Bible say, yeah! Yeah! *

Note

*"WE AND DEM"
Written by Bob Marley

Part Three
Echoes from a Troubled Land

My own ideal is a hollow dream,
My horizon the unforeseen
And I am homesick,
Homesick for a land I have not seen.

—Tristan Corbiere

15

Day Forty-One

The members of the Haitian diaspora were just waiting for an opportunity to display their sorrow. On that day, they were not just crying over the death of thirty-three fellow men, women, and children who had perished at sea; they were also protesting against the degradation of their estranged country. Many curious Haitians made the trip to Virginia Key that day. They came via taxi. They came via jitney. They all wanted to see with their own eyes what had become of their fellow men and women. In death, the refugees had succeeded in bringing the Haitian community together. In addition to that, they also secured Ben-X a ride into the community of Little Haiti. It turned out that he did not just have one family member or friend greeting him at his port of entry into the promised land—he had a whole community welcoming him. There were no police officers! No Immigration officers! For no one knew that he was part of the unfortunate group that had washed ashore. What a perfect cover! Ronald St. Fort was again the lone survivor. He would keep it that way for as long as he possibly could.

The radio stations opened their telephone lines to a riveted audience. The metropolitan Miami area had been transformed into a giant town hall. The Haitian Americans once again took the opportunity to express their anger at the lack of response from those who they believed had created the problem in the first place. Right in America's backyard, genocide was taking place and there was no government outcry. Thousands of people were being maimed, raped, and killed, and no one seemed upset. How close was the troubled land? Close enough for bodies to wash up on the beaches of sunny Miami. This catastrophic event had the effect of keeping the plight of the Haitians in the media for a couple of days. It warranted a couple of headlines and then . . . and then it was quickly forgotten. The sensation-hungry anchormen and women, along with the paparazzi, had moved on to other stories. The events had stricken a very sensitive nerve in the American conscience and no reporter dared to stay with such a topic. No connection was ever made between the coup in Haiti and the deaths of these unfortunate people.

In Little Haiti, Ben-X was like a fish in water. He hung around the church in the morning and was able to secure some help. In this land of plenty, being homeless was the easiest thing to do. You claim a corner. You place a few markers, such as an abandoned shopping cart, some cardboard, or any knick-knacks that you can get your hands on, and the corner is yours. When you are chased away, you simply move to the next corner. Never argue. Present yourself as a nice guy. Most of the homeless people are nice, anyway. It fits the profile. Ben-X even found out how to secure a clean bed to sleep in at night. He quickly became a regular at the St. Vincent Shelter. He had to be at the shelter by 7:00 P.M. No one ever asked him for any identification. He tried to draw as little attention as possible to himself.

The St. Vincent Shelter was like a large transient commune. The rules were very simple. Be there by 7:00 P.M. No pets allowed. A well-balanced meal was served by 8:00 P.M. On most nights, the 100-bed, indoor gymnasium was filled to capacity. It was quite an endeavor for the charitable agencies to offer assistance to the thousands of homeless people who seemed to be everywhere in the commercial section of Miami. However, restoring the homeless their dignity seemed to be a much more difficult task than merely providing food and shelter. Ironically, the country with the most vibrant economy in the world shared a common problem with the poorest country in the hemisphere. Was it a sign of personal failure, or a sign of the failure of a political system that could not plan and offer second chances to all of its citizens? Ben-X met entire families who, for whatever reasons, had found themselves completely deprived of the bare necessities of life. Would the homeless ever regain their sense of personal pride, their identities?

Ben-X followed all the rules and blended in well with the rest of the crowd. If it were not for his French accent and his difficulty with simple words like *water* and *work,* no one would have been able to distinguish him from the other homeless people. He was able to engage in some recreational activities. He learned about the American people's passion for sports like baseball and football. Some of the residents could go on for hours talking about how their favorite team had made it to the Super Bowl. The stories were embellished and transformed much like folktales. He also learned that if he ever had trouble at one shelter, he could always move to another one. Mr. Peterson, who came to St. Vincent after he had been evicted from another shelter for violating the rules, had done that.

16

How had Ronald St. Fort, aka Ben-X, developed such ability to survive? How had he become so resilient? He was born in Gonaives, a small coastal city with a glorious past of revolts against invaders and tyrants from both outside and within. The extremely dusty and dry land of Gonaives was surrounded by the slums of Raboteau. More recently, it was credited as being the place where the uprising against the antiquated Duvalier regime really took shape. Ben-X never knew his real parents, as he was given up at the age of four to Mr. and Mrs. Racine to live as a *restavek.* In their home, he learned firsthand how unkind his fellow humans could be.

As a *restavek,* Ronald was in charge of the early morning duties. He rose before anyone else, and gathered the bedpan, which held everyone's urine, vomit, and other disgusting excretions. He then emptied it in a nearby canal and rinsed the pot for later use. Next, he had to shine the shoes of Mr. Racine and Mr. Racine Jr. (a seven-year-old boy named Larry), and have them ready for work and school. Should Mrs. Racine find them not shiny enough for her liking, she often pushed Ronald's head down until his face touched the shoes.

"Can't you see that these shoes are not clean?" Mrs. Racine would scream in a rage. Ronald was never allowed to eat breakfast or have dinner at the table with the other children. He ate his dinner in the outside kitchen after Mrs. Racine's children had had enough. Often, he was beaten up with a rigwaz[1] because he had accidentally broken a plate or just because Mrs. Racine was having a bad day.

The *restaveks* were often kept out of school, as they were too busy with domestic work. Ronald had to accompany his master's son to school, carry his backpack, and refer to him as "Mr. Larry." Larry's mother was a brash woman who treated everyone in a demeaning manner. For eight years Ronald endured both verbal and physical abuse. He had been hit with shoes, belts, and anything else that was in arm's reach. Sometimes he was slapped just for daring to have an argument with Larry.

Mrs. Racine came from a very dysfunctional family who had lived with the dream of one day making it into the Haitian aristocratic class. The Racines were far from aristocrats. Never mind that Mrs. Racine could barely read and write, or that she had never left the town where she was born. She could not speak French but she would not allow herself to be caught speaking Creole, either. Mrs. Racine wanted to portray herself as Mrs. Etiquette. She enjoyed having barbecues, to which she would invite all the notables and affluent neighbors—who never showed up. She went to such extremes to make sure that everything was proper, that her guests could not help but laugh at her. "Get on with the food already, Mrs. Racine," one impatient and hungry guest once said. "Enough *tulututu*[2]—just pass the damn food!" Mrs. Racine never graduated from secondary school, and her grammar and pronunciation were very poor. She had the embarrassment of her life when one evening in front of all her guests, her nine-year-old daughter innocently tried to correct her grammatical error.

Mrs. Racine constantly reminded Ronald of his humble origins. One day, after Ronald and Larry got into a squabble over something, Ronald gave Larry one big blow to the chest. Ronald was tired of being blamed for everything that Larry did. He felt that he had nothing to lose.

Larry ran to his mother in tears.

"Mama, Mama, Ronald hit me," cried Larry.

It was quite a sight to see Larry, a chubby ten-year-old boy, whining after having been hit by an undernourished, skin-and-bones eight year old. Mrs. Racine was fuming.

"Ronald, come here. Right now!" she yelled across the room. She could be heard from a block away. She grabbed Ronald by the ear, held him in between those huge hams of hers, and delivered a long diatribe.

"Remember, *Ti gason,*"[3] Mrs. Racine would say, "that you are nobody. You hear me? Nobody? Your mother is nobody. Look at your fingers. Are they all the same length?"

"No," the eight-year-old Ronald would answer softly.

"Now you understand," Mrs. Racine continued, "Larry and you are not the same. Treat him with respect, or I will send you back where you came from." Ronald was petrified. For a moment he thought that this mad woman was going to hammer him into the ground. Maybe in her mind, she did. When a person pretends to be that high and mighty, wanting to be royalty when he or she is not, that person either has to stand on a hill at all times, or bury everyone else in the ground. Otherwise, his or her buffoonery becomes obvious to everyone.

Ronald had shed many tears that night. These tears, however, were not wasted. They were the leaven of hate, the leaven of courage and resolve that would help him to grow into a very determined man. Ben-X had a very open and analytical mind. It took him some time to ponder and examine all of the possibilities, but after he had made up his mind, no one could make him change it. Never would he be swayed from his determination to rid his country of the mold that had produced the Mrs. Racines by the thousands. Ronald heard these demeaning words over and over and grew resentful—not just of Mrs. Racine, but of the whole *restavek* system that would allow children like him to be put down and told that they were inferior and would never amount to anything.

As for Mr. Racine, he was a notary but liked to be referred to as *Maitre* Racine, as though he were an attorney. He had long lost interest in conjugal life, and it was common knowledge that his mistress, Francine, was the love of his life. Any time the subject was brought up, Mrs. Racine's blood pressure rose and Ben-X had to watch out. Mr. Racine contributed very little to Ben-X's upbringing. He was hardly seen around the house, but when he was home, everyone knew about it. He was there to enforce the rules and dish out punishment for the more serious infractions. When he was around, the usually loud and brash Mrs. Racine was always as docile as a lamb.

Notes

1. Goatskin whip.
2. Uppity attitude.
3. Little boy.

17

"One day," Ronald often thought to himself, "I will change this country and no one will be allowed to mistreat another human being—especially the children." Little did Mrs. Racine know that she was planting in this child's mind the seeds of revolutionary change. For he had been a child exposed to an overly oppressive environment. Such strong feelings of resentment would never go away. One way or another, these feelings were bound to spring up later.

These same feelings of resentment might explain the resolve and determination of the street children of Haiti who resorted to random violence to settle old scores. Their gripe was not with the apparently innocent middle class man or woman that they attacked . . . or maybe it was. Every day on the streets of Port-au-Prince, the homeless children tried to get back some of the innocence that they had never enjoyed but knew they were entitled to. These children have been robbed of the innocence and the playfulness that is so characteristic of their age. They wake up every day only to realize that their childhood has eluded them. Are they terrorists? No, not by a long shot. They are not terrorists because they are the true victims of a country that has abandoned them. They are like drifters in a society that has pushed them aside. They have fallen victim to the many lies issued from educators and politicians. Their schools failed to give them the tools that they needed to survive in a more and more hostile and competitive environment. They sent out distress calls but the politicians looked the other way.

There have been no legal steps taken to protect the Haitian children from exploitation. For far too long, they have gone to bed with empty stomachs, wondering when was the last time they had a good meal. They seek green pastures where they can run and play like children, but their country is fast becoming an ecological disaster. The trees are being destroyed. When these children become adults and are ready to take over, all they will have left will be the carcass of a country. Wherever they turn, they encounter anguish and desolation. They have no respite from the sweltering heat. They longed to hear the sounds of lullabies, but all they heard was the sound of bullets. They wanted to appreciate the beauty of the rising sun, but all they saw was a stream of blood—the blood of their own brothers, sisters, mothers, fathers, and friends. Long gone are the idyllic scenes of a united community built on mutual respect where neighbors help neighbors. The laughter of children playing in the park has been replaced by screams of panic. The Haitian Army has gone berserk and has declared war against its own people.

Today the children of the streets stand as accusers of all the leaders past and present. During their rule, these leaders have allowed their ship to drift into giant reefs, while they passively watched it sink to the bottom of the sea. The children are angry with these leaders for their silence. They are angry at the world for letting this system go on for too many days and too many nights. Every day on the streets of Port-au-Prince the *sans-logis*[1] youths stand as judge, jury, and executioner. These youths are the true victims because they have been made into ghosts of children that never were. Do not tell them about the Haitian society of yesteryear—they never belonged to it. Do not tell them about how the streets used to be safe, because they have never felt safe. Don't tell them about how it feels to be cuddled and loved by a caring mother, for they have never seen their mothers. On the streets of Port-au-Prince, they have tried to hold on to anything that would give them an identity and a sense of belonging. Without warning or preparation, they were thrust into a situation that they were too young to even comprehend. They learned to steal, break car windows, and even assault others to demonstrate their readiness and prove their worth. Do not tell them about their fathers, the heroes, for they do not know their fathers. They know nothing about respect for others, for they have never seen it in practice. All they have seen is cruelty, atrocity, and the viciousness of people who have discounted them as unimportant and unworthy of love or attention.

In many ways, the streets of Port-au-Prince have become a giant university without walls—a place where these children learned the only skills that they felt they needed to survive: to rob, to shoot, and to kill. Unfortunately, from this university will come the leaders, the coup makers, the *magouilleurs*,[2] and scam artists of the Haitian society of tomorrow. Whenever one child is destroyed or not allowed to grow and blossom, it is the future of the country that is being destroyed. Once the current generation of failed leaders is gone, who will lead the country?

Ronald St. Fort had grown very resentful of injustice in any shape or form. One day he decided that enough was enough. He left Mrs. Racine's home and never went back. He was only twelve years old. He started attending St. Joseph's Church on a regular basis and eventually became an altar boy. Through the Catholic Church, Mrs. Lespinasse offered to adopt him.

Mrs. Lespinasse was the exact opposite of Mrs. Racine. She was caring and nurturing, and insisted that Ronald receive a good education. Ronald attended private school and did very well. Soon he was at the top of his class. As an adolescent, Ronald dreamed of changing the world. He soon became very engrossed in the writings of Mao Zedong and Regis Debray. He was an avid student of the Cuban Revolution. He knew of the Chilean experience with Salvador Allende and the apparent involvement of the CIA and ITT in bringing down the leftist regime.

Ronald envisioned that one day he would change his own country. There would be no more children restaveks—it was a flagrant form of slavery. He envisioned a country in which everyone would be treated the same. He dreamed of a classless society. He became an avid student of Haitian history. He often wondered what would have become of Hispaniola and the rest of the New World, had it not been "discovered" by Christopher Columbus. He knew that the true story about this so-called discovery was waiting to be told. Ronald realized that he needed to look far beyond the current events to understand Haiti's problems. Haiti had been a victim of a huge conspiracy. Only when it became convenient for the United States did it finally recognize Haiti as a sovereign nation. It had even been reported that the U.S. government had planned to ship all the African-Americans to Haiti and Liberia around the time of Haiti's independence.

After the war of independence was fought and won, the leaders of the new nation were left with an enormous task: to convert a large feudal society into a nation. For Haiti had been such a wealthy fiefdom that it had earned France its membership into the "rich men's club." The only government models that the Haitian leaders had at that time were those of the countries of their former masters. These empires were still seeking new territories to exploit in order to soothe the insatiable appetites of the kings and emperors of Europe for gold and other resources. Since Haiti did not have the military might to invade other territories and become a colonial empire, the Haitian leaders turned inward and transformed the new nation of Haiti into a colony for their own benefit. This time, the exploiters were not French men from a remote land; they were Haitians. The former slaves would have very little to show for their freedom. They would remain in the fields where they would sweat and labor, while the landowners enjoyed life in the major cities or abroad. They became the masses, the peasants, the *moun an deyo,*[3] the first ones on the fields in the early morning hours, and the last ones to go home. They became the faceless people—the ones that the politicians would run to with *tafia*[4] and *bouyon presidan*[5] whenever election time neared. They were always quickly forgotten until the next election.

The same pattern had continued throughout Haitian history. The people worked from the wee hours of the morning until after sunset. They labored in the sweltering Caribbean tropics. They kept the grocery shelves well supplied with products too expensive for them to afford. They produced grade A meat, chickens, and eggs, but could not afford to eat it. Their children suffered from kwashiorkor and malnutrition, while they fed a whole country. In spite of all of this, they never complained. They asked for very little and very little has been given to them. They never demanded medical care, and none was provided for them. They suffered from diseases long eradicated from the civilized world. They had no idea that most of the diseases that killed them by the thousands were preventable. Some people said that they were better off not knowing because a little bit of knowledge can be dangerous. Yet, these same people sent *their* children to the best universities abroad.

Was there any difference between the present and the pre-independence era? Why should it matter to the masses whether the colonizers were foreigners or Haitians? Nothing had changed. Why would the oligarchy want the situation to change? Why would their partners from the multinational corporations want anything to change? Why offer better hospitals, better schools, and better housing when the masses had not even asked? Why would they want the masses to know that at the dawn of a new millennium, a life expectancy of forty-seven years is just not acceptable? Why would they want the status quo to ever change? The masses were more desirable as an unlimited source of cheap labor to be shifted from the bateys of the Dominican Republic to the sweatshops of cities thousands of miles away. Is it any surprise that whenever the status quo was threatened, the millionaires and corporation owners simply sponsored another coup? Is it any surprise that there were always enough mercenaries to execute their orders? Coups will continue to happen in Haiti, in Guatemala, in Sierra Leone, and in the Philippines. Haiti has had so many coups that historians and researchers have come to expect them. The excuse? "It is part of the culture. . . . " Same story, same scenario, same plot, some players, and . . . same victims. Whenever a faction of the oligarchy thought another faction had too much power, out it went. Coup number . . . "Ote-toi, que je m'y mette."[6] For the 193 years since Haiti's independence, there had been a succession of conspiracies aimed at asphyxiating the island nation. For different reasons, maybe, the technique of suffocation and asphyxiation used against Cuba had been used in Haiti for decades. . . .

There was no way a group of black ex-slaves was going to be allowed to build a successful nation. This model of a country would be based on no master plan, no ideology, but rather on the continuation of a system of exploitation of the resources of the country for the benefit of a few. The status quo had to be maintained at all cost. For the masses, not much had changed. The people no longer had French masters; they had Haitian masters. In the days following the war of independence, the forefathers, finding themselves victorious, faced a big question. "Now that we are a free nation, what are we going to do?" To this date, that question has not been satisfactorily answered. A statement from the American ambassador in the months preceding the last election epitomized the situation very well. "Apre bal tambou lou."[7] Once the euphoria and celebration that followed the Haitian independence were over, the burden of building a nation would be very heavy. One might even add that "Big Brother" would make sure that rocks weighing several tons were placed in the drum. The American sentiment seemed to be much the same as it had been earlier in the century, when an assistant secretary of state had said, "The Haitians are an inferior people unable to maintain the degree of civilization left to them by the French, or to develop any capacity of self government entitling them to international respect and confidence." In *The Haiti Files,* James Ridgeway presented even less flattering statements that had been made by high-ranking military officials who ruled Haiti during the occupation of 1915–1934. They used the "N" word over and over to describe the Haitians. From the time Haiti became independent, it had been stabbed in the back over and over. The leaders of the democratic worlds allied themselves time after time with the most brutal and barbaric Haitian dictators. The perpetrators had always been allowed to exit in style. Large war planes had always been sent to pick them up. They were allowed to take the money and run, and were congratulated for their "selflessness in helping resolve the crisis."

What crisis? A group of men committed atrocious crimes against humanity and they were allowed to get away. That is the real crisis. "A bloodshed has been avoided," the official self-congratulatory statement from the American officials said. Whose blood were they talking about? The people had already shed the blood. The blood of several thousands of innocent Haitian victims, to be exact. Ben-X was not going to count on a system that had been put in place by the enemies of the Haitian people to bring about justice. It was utopian to believe that it would be possible to one day see even one of the perpetrators of the crimes against the Haitian people brought to justice. There was one promise that Big Brother always seemed to keep: "You work for me, and no harm will come to you. No matter how bad the situation appears to be, do not despair. Big Brother keeps his word. Just be patient. Don't get nervous when a long list of indictments is drawn against you. It is only paper. Not to worry; Big Brother will take care of you."

Ben-X had seen it happen in Haiti, in other Latin American countries, in Africa, and elsewhere. The only exception to the rule might have been in the case of the colonel from Panama. Ben-X would be foolish to believe that this time things would be any different. As for the church, it would only call for justice when it was convenient to do so. The traditional church, as an establishment, had never been on the side of the Haitian people in their struggle. The traditional church never decried the abuses of the Duvalier regime and the other dictatorial provisional governments that followed. In fact, the authorities of the church seemed, at times, to be enjoying a lucrative partnership with the corrupt system. That approach had always been their modus operandi: Say nothing when the people are being killed; raise your "moral voice" when the people are trying to settle the score. They had allied themselves with the slave masters during slavery time, then with the landowners, and more recently with the Duvalier dictatorship. They always seemed to follow the smell of money. Trust their godly talk at your own risk. Not every bird that quacks like a duck is a duck. Not everyone who says godly words is necessarily godly. In Haiti, many prelates, including the head of the church, for many years never even attempted to disguise their affiliations with the dictatorial regime. The favorite sermon from one of the Macoute-priests during the Duvalier regime was, "Tout pouvoir vient de Dieu."[8] In other words, one should be docile and accept the abuse from the *Tonton Macoutes*. Should Ben-X have expected the judicial system to provide justice? Not a chance. Not when the justices had been appointed by the coup makers and seemed to share common interests with them. They had always practiced auction justice. May the party willing to pay more in kickbacks win!

Notes

1. Homeless.
2. Schemers.
3. Hillbillies.
4. Grain alcohol.
5. A party given by a candidate during an election.
6. "Move over, so I can sit."
7. "After the dance, the drums are heavy."
8. "All power comes from God."

18

What would Ben-X do? He took to heart the first line of Mao Zedong's little red book: "Know who your enemies are!" You'd better believe that Ben-X knew who his enemies were. The military men who were looting or keeping watch while the traditional pillagers were plundering the country: They were his enemies. More specifically, the gunmen who came to his mother's home that night and massacred his whole family: They were his enemies. The people who had plunged his country back into the Dark Ages, making it unlivable. The men who had made Haitians around the world the laughingstock of everyone. They were definitely his enemies.

Ben-X was a man without a country. His homeland had been taken over by a group of vile individuals who sold their souls and their humanity for money. Every day under that dictatorial regime, it was like flesh being pulled off an animal in agony. There were millions of people in pain—their sleep haunted by pictures of death and unclaimed bodies. Scores of fatherless and motherless children begged to get back a taste of naïveté. Chaos now ruled the land that their forefathers so valiantly fought to free. The people responsible for these scenarios were his enemies. The gunmen who roamed the streets of Haiti and made it impossible for children and families to grow and develop as human beings were his enemies . . . the enemies of humanity. The people responsible for the death of his fellow passengers on the sailboat *L'Espoir*: They were his enemies.

There was no place in the tormented world where Ben-X could find solace. He suffered from recurring flashbacks of hills of corpses. Everything around the man was falling apart. Death and desolation were all around him. He is the lone survivor. From that point forward, his whole life would be dedicated to the pursuit of justice and the fulfillment of a promise he had made to his mother, his brother, and sisters, and, more recently, to his fellow passengers on *L'Espoir*. The souls of his fellow men and his family members were begging for justice. Who would quench this thirst for justice that was in the heart of every Haitian?

So far, it had been a very unbalanced war. One side had the Uzis, the .44 Magnums, the M-16s, and the machine guns. Were they warriors or terrorists? They were a little bit of both. They were ready to exterminate all of their enemies and they were guided by no rules. Their victims were left without recourse. The other side had only its will to survive and the determination to resist until the very last breath. The score was unbalanced, with thousands of victims on one side and none on the other side. How could anyone think about peace and harmony without justice? How could anyone think about closure without recognition of guilt?

Ben-X felt that he had all the justification that he needed to embark on an extremely risky sojourn. He would become judge, jury, and executioner of every single person he found responsible for thwarting the efforts of the Haitian people to survive as citizens of a free nation—citizens with full rights. Who would come forward and take responsibility for the genocide that was happening?

> Fok nou fe jistis pou fre-n yo
> Ki tonbe anba grif tig yo.
> Piyaje ak kriminel yo

dwe jije pou move zak yo.
—Pierre Antoine Jules, Sanba Lele*

We must demand justice for our brothers
Who fell under the claws of the tigers.
Pillagers and criminals
Must be put on trial for their misdeeds.
—Pierre Antoine Jules, Sanba Lele*

Ben-X would fulfill this promise no matter what the cost, no matter what the sacrifice. Even death could not and would not stop him. He had one mission: to find every killer and make him pay. Ben-X took a white piece of paper, pricked his left middle finger with a pin, and, with a drop of blood, inscribed the word *justice* in bold letters. He then lit the paper with a match and watched it go up in flames until all the letters disappeared. The vow had been sealed. The quest for justice was under way . . .

For months, Ben-X was haunted by the pictures he saw on television. He saw faces that he recognized in spite of the disfiguration caused by the seawater and shark bites. Ronald was supposed to have been one of them, but he was not. He would have to live with this fact for the rest of his life. He often woke at night with panic attacks. He would see himself fighting under the water with a giant white shark. He would always wake up at the moment when the shark was about to swallow him. This had happened so many times that he was no longer afraid. Somehow, the story of his life was being replayed over and over in this dream. He often blamed himself for being alive. But he was grateful. He saw a hidden meaning in all of this.

Why was his life spared? He was still alive because he had a mission. Maybe he could cheat the course of history.

*Used by permission of Pierre A. Jules.

Maybe he could win a few ones for the Haitian people. The Haitians always seemed to be on the losing end. The Haitians were immediately assumed to be economic rather than political refugees. Thousands of asylum seekers were being arbitrarily sent away to Guantanamo, Cuba, pending deportation to a land that had been transformed, according to the most reputable accounts, into a "killing field." If you were white or if you could serve America as a propaganda tool, America was still the promised land. But whenever Haitians came close enough to the land of the free, they were kept in captivity in places like Krome Detention Center. If they were too young and caused an embarrassment for the highly moralistic and puritan American public, the children were sent to remote places like Jackson, Mississippi. It was not enough that they had been uprooted from their country and whatever was left of their families. Now they had to live in unfamiliar surroundings. At no time in American history had any child received such treatment from the government. At least no white children had.

Ben-X would have to use all his ingenuity to remain undetected. He had no intention of living in captivity in a modern concentration camp. The barbed wires were there. Restriction of movement was part of the policy. The lack of hope and the fear of being sent back into the hands of their torturers contributed to create an atmosphere similar to a Nazi antechamber where Jews and other prisoners were waiting to be sent to the gas chambers. He was not going to get caught. Disguising himself as a homeless person was the easiest thing to do. There were so many of them in the area. He became familiar with the times when the major restaurants of the area would dispose of the leftovers. He and his homeless peers would converge on the large dumpsters like scavengers. Ben-X came to know firsthand how much food was being wasted in a land where significant numbers of children and elderly still went hungry.

He found plenty of food and much more. He was now the proud owner of a small transistor radio. A little bit of tinkering here and there, and he was connected to the world. He sought refuge in churches but never told his real story to anyone. He became known as Ron, the nice fellow who was always ready to lend a helping hand to whoever would ask. Smooth, polite, approachable, and educated, homeless Ron was not any different from the majority of homeless people that he met. He found out that the great majority of them were not hoodlums on the run, escapees from mental institutions, or misfits. They were people like Brian, an ex-college literature professor who could not recover from his divorce.

Brian quickly caught Ben-X's attention. For some reason he seemed out of place on the street corner.

Brian came to Ben-X, a cigarette hanging out of the corner of his mouth, and said, "Do you have a light, brother?" Ben-X did not quite understand what he said, but gathered that he wanted a match.

"I do not have any light, Mr.—"

"Call me Brian!" he said. Brian was very articulate. He spoke very clearly and distinctly, making it easier for Ben-X to pick up the meaning of the words. From what Ben-X could figure out, Brian had been an English professor at a community college. He got involved in a very nasty divorce with his wife. Not only had he lost his home, but he also lost his wife, his daughter, and most of his friends. It was so painful for him to see his daughter cry when his weekly visits were over, that he stopped attempting to see her. He had not seen them since he moved to Miami more than three years ago. He had lost all faith in a justice system that would treat fathers so unfairly. He took to drinking to drown his chagrin and could never get back on his feet.

John's story was as poignant as Brian's was. A man of great athletic abilities, John seemed destined for greatness. He succeeded in every sport that he entered. He had already won the state championship in track and field three times. He was such a fast 100-meter runner that he had earned the nickname, "Speedy John." He nourished great hope for a medal at the Los Angeles Olympics in 1984, but was eliminated in the final heat when he fell and broke his ankle. He became so depressed that he withdrew from everyone. He attempted to kill himself at least three times. All that those attempts earned him was a quick trip to and a short stay at the County Hospital Crisis Center, with the stigma and humiliation attached to it. He had since given up on suicide, too. He is now very philosophical about the idea of death, often stating to whomever wants to listen, "I was robbed by everyone, including death." Homeless Ron had many similarly interesting stories to tell, but he could not afford to blow his near-perfect cover. As it appeared, homeless people were such outcasts that it was unlikely for Immigration officials to look for illegal aliens amongst them.

19

The news from Haiti continued to be very revolting. Atrocities were reported that would have made even the Gestapo officers cringe. The international community reacted swiftly to condemn the coup. The United States flip-flopped many times. At times, it seemed to show total support for the restoration of the deposed constitutional government. At other times, it was more busy cow towing to the coup makers, confirming in the minds of a very vocal diaspora that the United States had been co-author, or at least co-conspirator in the *coup d'état*. The members of the *de facto* regime in Haiti, backed by a full blitz of international media, were being more sleek in the way they proceeded to break the spine of the opposition. Youths, *syndicat*, and union leaders were kidnapped and were not heard from anymore. It was rumored that they were often tied up with heavy cement blocks and thrown into the sea. The officers of the Haitian Army and their *attachés* were so arrogant. Any time the international community placed another restriction on the pariah regime, the military men would react with more repression. Roadblocks were put up almost every day. Suspects were pulled out of their cars and executed summarily. Arrogance and cruelty with impunity were the order of the day.

While the media were focusing on Lieutenant Colonel Franklin, other officers became jealous and started to build reputations of their own. Certain names started to come up frequently on the daily news bulletins. Colonel Ambroise became famous for his interrogatory techniques. He would tie all the extremities of his prisoner together to a center post and spin the prisoner around while he was hit with a makeshift baton or a four-by-four. Captain St. Hilaire's specialty was to pull the mustache and the beard of his victim with a pair of tweezers that he kept in a container of hot pepper sauce. He would ask questions with double meanings to confuse his subjects and each time he received what he determined to be the wrong answer, he would pull a lock of hair. Captain Larose, nicknamed "Dan Gryin" because he seemed to be always laughing, took immense pleasure in having his prisoners beaten up on the soles of their feet and then forcing them to walk. He would deride his victims, laughing with his cronies while drinking Rum Barbancourt. "Sak pase a pa ou pa kab mache? Kouri pito? Ha, ha, ha . . ." "What is happening? You cannot walk? Why don't you run instead?"

Little did those torturers know that in Ben-X's (homeless Ron's) mind, they were signing their own death sentences. Ben-X was absorbing every bit of the information like a sponge. He had discreetly accumulated a dossier on every one of these officers and their accomplices. Ben-X was saddened but not surprised to see highly educated professionals jumping on the bandwagon to justify the mess into which the country had been plunged. The coup makers found a very articulate spokesperson in a female attorney nicknamed by the diaspora, "the CNN bigmouth of Petionville." Any time CNN needed a sound bite, there she was, perched on the hills with the beautiful bay of Port-au-Prince in the background. She had been made into an expert of the Haitian Constitution, international law, and of everything that a CNN reporter needed to concoct a credible story line. It seemed that this lawyer was on a one-woman mission to bring down single-handedly the whole democratic movement. She was at every demonstration of the ultra right, and she had the eloquence to support her antiquated view that isolationism and a false sense of nationalism that would benefit only the oligarchy were defendable. That view, in essence, was full of contradictions, since she was suggesting that the great majority of the people, the masses, be left out of the equation. Needless to say, the conservative branch of the U.S. media quickly embraced those views. Brigadier General Tobias and his followers were almost depicted as heroes who would save Haiti from the proverbial red revolution and a "wacko president with very undemocratic ways." The usual "Jim Crows" in American politics led the charges with flip charts at hand.

Ben-X was not surprised because there was a lot of money to be made out of this chaos. It all seemed ironic that fortunes were being made while the nation was under an economic embargo. Coming out in support of the coup so forcefully was a ticket to a share of the black market. These intellectuals had never supported any changes, anyway. In a changed society, their bluffs would be called, and they would have to demonstrate and apply what they really knew at the service of the country. Maybe their parents would have been very disappointed to find out that all of the money they spent sending their sons and daughters to European and other foreign universities was all for naught—that the diplomas issued by the board of trustees of the Sorbonne or Universidad Autonoma de . . . were worthless and irrelevant in a country like Haiti. Maybe these university graduates stood a better chance to make money by scamming and conning while talking Parisian French or English mixed with Ebonics to impress a nation close to 85 percent illiterate. The situation in Haiti was a golden opportunity. These men had been sent abroad to study by their Duvalierist parents, and they had come back to find a country in transition. The coup in process gave them an opportunity to rise and shine. It was their status quo. What choice did they have but to support it?

The more arrogant and supercilious the killers in Haiti sounded, the more Ben-X wanted them to pay. So far, the coup makers had been undisturbed. There were rumors that members of the resistance had received training in Kadhafi's Libya and that an armed resistance was about to start. There were even rumors of a guerilla group activated in the northern part of the country. It was just another excuse for the Haitian Army to mount a huge search-and-destroy military operation. Hundreds of unarmed and innocent civilians lost their lives.

Had the leaders of the resistance seriously considered modern urban guerilla warfare, or were they just words of comfort to a resistance that was quickly losing all hope? In the final analysis, the strong men in Haiti did not seem to be overly bothered or frightened by the prospect of finally having someone actually shoot back at them. Ben-X's guess was that they would probably run. It is easy to look like GI Joe and Rambo when the people on your side are the only ones with the machine guns, the M-16s, and the concussion grenades. The officers of the army did not lose any sleep over the prospect of armed confrontation. Their well-informed sources had probably tipped them off that they did not have a thing to worry about. If any sources of annoyance were going to come to any of the officers, they would have to come from a one-man army that would perform surgical strikes on selected targets. This called for a man who was not afraid to die for a cause. It would take a man who was driven by a burning desire to see justice done. It would take a man like Ben-X. From now on, every minute of every day would be used to prepare for this mission.

Ben-X's adaptation to Miami life was progressing very well. He had even been able to perform some odd jobs for a few dollars. He bought some clothes and sported a more presentable appearance. He did not want to look too fancy, since that would raise suspicion about who he really was. He just wanted to look kempt enough not to turn off prospective employers. Through the shelter counselors, Ben-X learned that recruiters for labor pools would sometimes come around looking for muscular looking males to load ships in the harbor. That was exactly the kind of job that Ben-X was looking for.

20

Ben-X was finally picked up one morning. He lifted hundreds of sacks loaded with food items and stacked them neatly in the holding area of the ship whose destination was Haiti. The embargo was a joke. This ship's name was St. Philomene but it could have easily been Embargobuster. At the end of the twelve-hour day, Ben-X was eighty dollars richer—ten dollars had gone to the recruiter. Welcome to America's underground economy. No questions asked. No papers checked. Bring your physical strength and your muscles and we will give you work. Just keep your mouth shut. The instructions from the recruiters were very direct. If Ben-X ever ran his mouth about what he'd seen on the boat, he was as good as dead.

This served Ben-X's interest and purpose just fine. He was in the right environment to collect a lot of intelligence about his future targets. The amount of information one could collect from seamen was unbelievable. He learned the names of the contact people on both sides of the smuggling operation. He also noticed that at certain times of the day, no temporary laborers were allowed on the ship. Certain areas of the ship were off limits, unless you wanted to get roughed up by the armed guards. One day, Ben-X feigned ignorance and went right past a red double door with the sign:

Authorized Personnel Only.
No Trespassing.

An angry guard quickly stopped him.

"Hold it . . . Man, can't you read the f . . . sign?"

"I'm sorry," Ben-X said timidly. Ben-X was a master at playing dumb. He could be very unassuming at times and had a way of dropping his shoulders and taking a very inoffensive posture. It worked. The irate man was almost apologetic. "I am just following orders, OK?" said the man. What could they possibly be hiding on this ship?

Ben-X did not know enough English to hold lengthy conversations, but he understood almost everything. He could, however, speak Spanish fluently, although no one had known. He had not chosen to volunteer any information. He was hoping that he could eavesdrop on some information, especially from these Hispanic-looking men who had visited the ship several times.

"Hablo con el comandante en Puerto Principe. El no es contento con la tardanza," Ben-X heard one of the men say. He had not mentioned any names and it was difficult to find out which *comandante* he was referring to. In a country in chaos, a *comandante* could be anyone. The Miami River area was abuzz with activities. It looked like a lot of ships were suddenly competing for the lucrative route. Temporary labor was plentiful. Ben-X was being picked up almost every day now. When one ship was at sea, he would work on a different ship. The competition was so fierce that seamen from one ship were badmouthing other ships. Ben-X learned that most weapons and ammunition sent to the putschists in Haiti were shipped out of this Miami River and that the St. Philomene sent more than arms. "When the time comes," Ben-X thought, "St. Philomene seems like the ship to be on."

Ben-X made sure he remained available to work on the St. Philomene at every opportunity. He would need to learn every corner and every possible hiding place on that ship. He befriended the foreman and volunteered for cleaning duties. Pretty soon he was circulating almost freely on the ship. All kinds of vehicles, including pickup trucks, larger trucks, and a few luxurious four-wheel drive utility trucks were sent to Haiti almost on every trip. They were always well covered and no one ever looked inside them after they were loaded on the ship. Maybe there were just too many to be inspected each time. Ben-X would remember that. The stocking area was noted to be extremely hot at all times. Surviving in this temperature would necessitate a lot of drinking water. Ben-X would have to take care of that in due time.

He did not give up his status as homeless Ron. It was almost like a badge of honor to be homeless in Ben-X's situation. While the immigration officials were mistreating his fellow Haitians and were implementing an obviously racist policy toward them, Ben-X took great pleasure in rubbing the noses of the officials in the mud. He was able to remain undetected. In spite of all of the resources that were being committed to making the life of unfortunate human beings miserable, he, Ben-X, was able to live incognito. It had been almost nine months. He had managed not just to survive. He had earned money and had enough to afford rent on a small room, but it would be taking unnecessary risks. "Why not leave well enough alone?" Ben-X thought to himself. The racist people must have known that, if given the opportunity, the minorities would outshine them. Maybe that is why they spent so much energy keeping the minorities under check. Who would think that Ben-X could have survived so much adversity and still be in a position to take on more challenges? His ability to immerse himself into Miami life was quite a feat. Somehow it had the sweet taste of revenge.

Now that Ben-X had a few hundred dollars, he decided that it would be advantageous to try to make some contact with whatever was left of his network of friends in Haiti. Some of the reporters were able to send coded messages and had been keeping track of the whereabouts of the officers. They knew where they hung out to drink, play cards, and gamble. The days and times they visited their mistresses had been carefully noted. In a small country living on the edge, very few activities were possible. Life, therefore, even for the richest and the most powerful, was very predictable. Get up late, go to the office for a couple of hours, and check on your drugs, gasoline, and other smuggling operations. Go to the beach with one of your mistresses and then set up for a long evening of besigue or poker in which large sums of money would be changing hands. If there is any hot spot on the check board, give orders to your cronies to go and take care of it immediately. Just another day in the tropics. Nothing exciting. Nothing unusual about this picture except that while everyone else seemed to be having a difficult time coping with the state of undeclared war, a select number of officers from the Haitian Army were amassing immense fortunes estimated in the millions of dollars.

Every army officer had turned into an importer and distributor of essential items like gasoline, rice, flour, and cooking oil. They held the Uzi in one hand and the cash box in the other. They were killing a portion of the population while trying to extort money from the rest, transforming the country into a giant black market. The population was kept under the gun, forced to buy rice and oil from the black marketers or starve to death. They had no place to go . . . nowhere to run. One would think that a people in bondage like the Haitians would cry uncle and accept the *fait accompli.*

Month after month Haitians from all over the world protested. They took to the streets. They blocked expressways. They went on a fax campaign. They circulated petitions. Ben-X kept a low profile and resisted the temptation to jump into the fray and make his opinion known. Some of the signs he read did catch his attention, though.

**General Tobias to be indicted
for genocide and rape of democracy.**

Ben-X did not participate in the demonstrations because technically, he did not exist. He was not supposed to be there. The members of the opposition to the de facto regime did what members of the opposition usually do best. They talked and talked and took no decisive action. The members of the resistance inside Haiti were waiting for some kind of bold and spectacular action that would embolden them to start a popular uprising. No such action came. Instead, a new group under the leadership of a CIA-supported, saber-waving, delirious, speech-making man was created to terrorize the population in a more systematic way. Only one side was acting scared and it was not the coup makers. The embargo was like Swiss cheese. Business was flourishing. A new breed of arrogant, *tete boeuf*[1] driving *nouveaux riches* were born. Meanwhile, the Organization of American States made resolution after resolution but took no action.

The Haitian-American radio stations served as round-the-clock hotlines where the Haitians could vent their anger about what they understood to be a huge conspiracy against Haiti. One of the radio hosts went as far as to interview live the *officier du jour* from the Police Headquarters in Haiti. The community became divided and polarized. Would the elected government of Haiti return to power or not? The rival factions were engaged in a public relations war. Some very vocal talk show hosts were killed under suspicious circumstances. But the voice of oppressed Haitians everywhere could not be silenced.

Haitian protests continued relentlessly. The community-based organization doubled as an information clearinghouse. All one needed to do to learn the latest news about Haiti was to hang out in Little Haiti. Ben-X gained access to news bulletins about every political activity in Haiti. Who was working from the inside? Who was working on both sides? Who had switched sides? Ben-X had vengeance on his mind. He did not trust that the international community was serious about restoring some degree of humanity and decency in Haiti. The delegates from the international agencies seemed at times more concerned about making nice with the putschists than pressuring them into making concessions. There were too many false starts, too many fudged meetings between the factions at war for Ben-X to expect that he would get some justice any time soon. Something was very fishy about an American war ship being kept from fulfilling its mission by a small group of locals brandishing flags and small-caliber rifles.

It had been three months since Ben-X had started to work on the ships at the Miami River. He had collected a lot of information on the schedules of these ships and the kind of cargo they were transporting. He considered sneaking aboard different ships, but decided on the St. Philomene. It was much bigger than the others were. Besides, Ben-X had definite proof that arms and ammunition were being transported on this ship. Every Wednesday at about 3:30 P.M., the ship was visited by a Colombian man called Juan. If only he could hear what they were discussing behind those doors. He wanted to know what was going on and did not mind taking a risk toward that end. He managed to hide in the ventilation system and was able to hear most of the dialogue that went on at one of the Wednesday meetings.

Juan looked particularly upset that day.

"Mierda," started Juan. *"Si usted no puede entregar la mercancia a tiempo, nosotros tendremos que buscar otro capitan."*[2]

"No se preocupe; yo lo hare,"[3] said a frightened Mr. Jean-Pierre, the captain of St. Philomene.

"Mi jefe no tolerara mas cagadas," continued Juan. *"La ultima vez se perdieron 500 kilos . . . yo quiero mi hijueputa dinero . . . Se este cargamento no llega alla a tiempo, el comandante lo hara pagar con su cabeza. A ellos se les esta acabando la amunicion."* (My boss will not tolerate any more screwups. Last time we lost 500 kilos . . . I want my fucking money. If this shipment does not arrive on time, the comandante will have your head. They are running out of ammunition.")

Jean-Pierre felt very threatened by that last statement. He knew exactly what Juan meant. Jean-Pierre felt under a lot of pressure to deliver this time. He cringed at the idea of ending up in a ditch with his throat sliced Columbia-necktie style. It had happened to Abner. Jean-Pierre once again promised himself that he would get out of the business soon. A couple more runs and it would be over. Jean-Pierre was in total denial of the fact that no one got out of that line of business. You don't just write a letter of resignation stating, "Dear Boss, it was nice doing business with you. I am afraid to die and I have decided to quit." You actually have to die or end up in jail for a long time—unless, of course, you became an informant and allow the authorities to catch a bigger fish. If you are lucky, you might be allowed to live somewhere in another city under a new identity. That amounted to being dead, anyway.

Jean-Pierre knew all of this; but greed was clouding his judgment. He would probably not stop. The smell of money had that addictive virtue to it and no one ever wants to stop making money. Money is what runs the world. It was the real cause of the atrocities and the mass murders being committed in Haiti. It was the reason why Jean-Pierre was risking his life on this boat on the Miami River, only miles away from the Miami Federal Court building where life sentences were being dished out every day.

As far as Ben-X was concerned, St. Philomene was definitely the ship to get on. It already had a reputation for losing some of its merchandise. Should any of the weapons be missing, the captain and his crew would be blamed. From what he gathered from the conversation between Juan and Jean-Pierre, the deadline was drawing to a close. St. Philomene could pull out of the harbor at any time. Ben-X had better be on it. The question now was when should he hide on the ship? Would he have enough time to put his affairs in order? He had become close to Speedy John and Brian, the two homeless men he'd met in downtown Miami. Behind their disheveled appearances and strong body odors were very thoughtful and profound human beings. They didn't ask much of anyone, and were always ready to share their human warmth and experience with anyone in need. Ben-X would choose them over General Tobias or Lieutenant Colonel Franklin anytime.

Ben-X needed to collect a few items that he would need for his journey. One never knows how long a trip will take. Sometimes a ship had to wait in high seas until the appropriate contact people on shore had given the all-clear signal. Not that anyone would dare stop a ship on the way to the pirate country of Haiti, once it had cleared the international waters. However, docking at the wrong time might mean making unbudgeted in-kind gifts to some snooping army officers. After what he heard from Juan, Jean-Pierre certainly could not afford that. Getting on the ship and finding a hiding place was extremely dangerous. It was even more dangerous for Ben-X to plan to rip the crew off of some of their precious cargo.

Notes

1. "Beef head": referring to the Toyota logo on the four-wheel drive utility cars.
2. "Shit. If you can't deliver the merchandise on time, we'll have to find another captain."
3. "Don't worry; I will be on time."

Part Four

Amongst Modern-Day Pirates

The first slaves were made so by force; the state of slavery was perpetuated by cowardice.
—Jean-Jacques Rousseau

21

Day 595

Ben-X arrived at work that day at the usual time, but this time his usual duffel bag was particularly heavy. He had acquired a few essential items, including a good flashlight, some over-the-counter antidiarrhetic medicine, some chlorine tablets, some Tylenol tablets, some Band-Aids, and a Swiss army knife. He had studied the plan of the ship over and over and had memorized every turn, every corner. He had identified where the main water supplies were. He even knew where consumable food items were stored.

St. Philomene was quite large. It stood with an LOA of 113 feet. It had been commissioned originally under the Liberian flag. It later became part of a large Panamanian fleet until a few years previous, when it was acquired by a group of investors that included some Haitian and Colombian nationals. It used to make two trips per month, but with the recent embargo of Haiti, business had been booming. The number of trips had been increased to three, which was very taxing to the relatively small crew. St. Philomene stood on the river like a small island almost the side of a football field. Ben-X did not know the exact capacity of the hull storage area, but it had taken as much as a week to fill up the space. Loading a ship is not as easy as it might look. It takes some special skills to perform the job, as the weight needs to be distributed evenly on both sides.

A pair of heavy-duty Caterpillar 12 engines that created a deafening noise powered the ship. St. Philomene was not a leisure ship and did not come with any of the amenities one would expect from a ship of that size. Its 750-gallon tank was always filled. A pair of mechanics were on board at all times and knew everything about the inner workings of the engines. A cook that doubled as a supply man kept the crew of eight well fed, judging by the size of everyone's waist. No one looked as if they had ever missed a meal. There was, of course, Captain Jean-Pierre. No one knew when and how he became involved in the business, but he appeared to be a very knowledgeable man who exuded respect and confidence. He was a natural leader. He was well liked by his subordinates and everyone seemed very loyal to him. What a difference between him and the late Captain Fombrun. At the end of the day, after collecting his pay, Ben-X did not get off the ship. He had a sudden urge to go to the bathroom and never came back out. The ship was a very busy place around payroll time. No one missed Ben-X. The ship had already been inspected and cleared.

In this line of business, cultivating the appropriate connections was extremely important. Such connections had to be on both sides. Judging by the summary inspection that St. Philomene had received, the ship owners were very well connected on the Miami side, too. Nothing to declare? Nothing to declare.

Ben-X needed to hang loose until he reached his final hiding spot. He had made up his mind about hiding in one of the large diesel trucks. After they were loaded, no one ever went to them, since they were very difficult to access. Ben-X wore a plain black T-shirt and a pair of black Levi's jeans. A black knit cap completed his outfit. These somber colors made him very difficult to detect in the poorly lit hallways of the ship. Ben-X had learned to move as stealthily as a ninja. Surviving the trip undetected promised to be interesting. Ben-X was driven by a high degree of self-confidence, without which it would be almost unimaginable for anyone to take on such an arduous and dangerous challenge. If caught, he would have a most difficult time explaining why he was on this ship en route to a place from which people by the thousands were trying to escape. He could always play dumb and explain that he had fallen asleep on board and did not know that the boat was going to leave. However, this still was an extremely dangerous prospect, since Jean-Pierre would most likely turn him over to his friends, the de facto authorities in Haiti.

Impossible; no way was he going to let that happen. The master of disguise had not survived so many adversities to have such a lackluster end. For a moment, Ben-X became quite anxious and his heart started to pound. A constant stream of memories from his whole life flashed right in front of his eyes. He saw the abuse he had endured from Mrs. Racine—the beatings and the life of deprivation he had suffered. He realized that nothing had ever come easy to him. Oftentimes he had had to take hold of his own life and had taken major risks. For almost two years he had been a man on the run. He was a fugitive from his native country. No indictments had been brought against him. They could not have been. Under what charges would he have been held? However, when an army was ruling by the force of the gun and the bayonet, why would it need any charges? Finding a long list of charges was the easiest part of the army's job. The judges had been instructed to emit a warrant for Ben-X's arrest for subversion of the security of the state. What an irony. The only people who had subverted the security of the Haitian people were the army itself and its cronies. If wishing to see the rights of his fellow Haitians restored was a crime, then yes, Ben-X was a criminal. If standing up to the killers and saying, "no more indiscriminate killings" was a crime, then by all means Ben-X was a criminal. If turning the tables and making every officer of the Haitian Army feel like a fugitive was a crime, let Ben-X be a criminal. If getting back into the lion's den and confronting the people who had exterminated his family was a crime, Ben-X definitely wanted to be a criminal.

Being named such a criminal was a title that he would relish. It was a badge of honor that Ben-X would wear with a lot of pride. It was a sign of valor that Ben-X would not mind sharing with every single one of the 6,500,000 Haitians. Accomplishing the mission that he had delineated for himself would be extremely difficult. But it was a mission that Ben-X had prepared for his whole life. He remembered his days in revolutionary Cuba. There he had learned that fighting his enemy necessitated first and foremost the political conviction that an injustice had been done. One needed to go beyond the single event itself. If a symbolic meaning to the event could be found, if the event could be seen as symptomatic of the larger problem of oppression of the people, then and only then was it a cause worth embracing. Ben-X had put the situation in Haiti to this very test over and over in his mind and had come up with the same resounding result. There was something awfully wrong with a whole country being held under the military boots of a few profiteers.

The next step was to choose a feasible response. Would it be a symbolic response? Would it be a response that would be more of an annoyance for the enemy but would not hurt it? Would it be a more powerful response, a response that would include the termination of key members amongst the enemies? Such a response would instill in the enemy for the first time some degree of fear, and might even make the surviving members of the enemy camp retreat from more blatant abusive practices. In other words, the latter method would give to the enemy a dose of its own medicine. It would be like looking the enemy right in the face and telling him, "Mr. Killer, it is your turn to be scared!" To have an impact the targets could not be random.

The next step was to estimate the cost in enemy reaction, should you succeed or fail. You have to decide whether or not you want the responses to appear like the work of a group or the work of a lone avenger. In the first case, there might be panic in the enemy camp and more repressive acts. In the second case, the strike might be discounted as random. In either case, the purpose of the strike is to put the enemy on the defensive and deter him from engaging in blatant acts of barbarism. In the situation at hand, if a strike could make any of the killers refrain from going on a killing rampage it would be worth it. It would be immoral to kill for personal property or personal material gain.

The last, but not least, step was to have the necessary resources to successfully complete the operation. This was usually the easiest step, because in a country that venerates the power of the gun, there were always plenty of opportunities. The enemy must be struck with his own spear. Ben-X had reviewed those steps in his head over and over during the past few months and had been tempted to let bygones be bygones, but each time there would be an incident to remind him how cruel and barbaric his enemy was. It was, indeed, a bitter cup from which he was about to drink, but one he felt he could no longer avoid. The blood of his comrades was crying for justice. He remembered the words that have been haunting humanity since the first murder ever committed. And the Lord, talking to Cain, said, "What have you done? Listen; your brother's blood is crying out to me from the ground! And now you are cursed from the ground, which has opened its mouth to receive your brother's blood from your hand. When you till the ground, it will no longer yield to you its strength; you will be a fugitive and a wanderer on the earth . . ."

The blood of Ben-X's young, innocent sisters was calling for justice. Ben-X was consumed with an intense and burning desire to fulfill the promises he had made to his deceased family members, to the memory of his fellow passengers on *L'Espoir,* and to himself. All he knew was that his native land had been transformed into something less than a civilized country. No longer was a human life valued. All traces of humanity had suddenly disappeared from the nation once so proud and ready to share his taste for liberty with all the sister nations of the Americas. To Ben-X, the situation his country was confronting was an ultimate call to duty. And there was no life too precious, no sacrifice too big, and no risk too great that was not worth taking in order to achieve the goal of restoring some dignity to the daily life of his fellow men. Ben-X was ready to carry out his duty one killer at a time, no matter the cost. No longer did he want to run away from the struggle of his people; no longer was he going to let his enemies claim victory for every single battle in the undeclared war between the rogue Haitian Army and the Haitian people. It was time that the enemy started to suffer some casualties.

All alone in the world, having lost his family, many of his comrades, and his tranquility, Ben-X felt that it was better that he act alone. He could not stand the thought of bringing other people into this quest, since the outcome was so uncertain. Should the bell finally toll for Ben-X, he wished for no long epitaph, no long procession of flower bearers. He would want to be remembered as someone who believed in equality and justice for all, and was willing to put his own life on the line to turn his belief into practice. Like any warrior, his secret wish was that the quest for freedom would continue and that someone would pick up the struggle where he left off. Why should there be any tears? Why should there be any eulogy? His fallen comrades had never received any. Their surviving relatives still could not mourn their passing. Ben-X was very aware of the danger he was facing. For the time being, however, he had a more urgent task at hand. He needed to survive the journey back home on a ship aboard which he was not supposed to be. Ben-X imagined that the ventilation system would be a safe place to wait until he was able to make his way to the truck. He decided to stay put for a while. The less he moved, the better he would be.

Ben-X did not know how long he had been in his current position. He must have fallen asleep. Was he dreaming, or was the ship moving? Was it the final call out to sea, or were the crew members just warming up the engine? Ben-X was in no position to find an answer to this question. What difference would it make, anyway? He could not move. He just would have to wait for other indications. He looked at his black *Sports Illustrated* promotion watch. It read 11:00 P.M. It was a little more than four hours since Ben-X had boarded that ship.

His eyes were quickly adjusting to the obscurity around him. Through a hole in the aluminum structure, Ben-X could distinguish everything inside the room below him. There were some rags, a mop, a large bucket, and ropes rolled in a pile. Regardless of what was happening with the boat, Ben-X figured it would be best to check things out later, when everyone would be preoccupied with hitting the sack. He would do it after midnight.

Things seemed particularly quiet. The ship was definitely moving. Maybe they had left the harbor after all. Indeed, they had. Ben-X came out of his hiding place and quickly realized that when at sea, the ship would be a very isolated place. There were just not enough people on this cargo ship for two people to meet, unless they had actually planned it. That was a bit of good news. Ben-X would remain on his toes, and avoid any unnecessary risks.

22

Ben-X was a very principled man. He could make do with very little. He moved with very resolute steps, his sneakers barely touching the ground. A few more steps straight ahead and Ben-X would make it to the side of the ship. He needed to have a good idea of what the exact situation was. He moved swiftly behind the supporting pillars of the ship and was able to take a good look at the scene. He could see the landscape of downtown Miami with all its glittering lights quickly vanishing into the darkness of the night. It was for real. The journey back home had just started. Adieu, Miami! Adieu, Little Haiti! Adieu, Haitian diaspora in Miami. Adieu, Immigration officers! *Veni, Vidi,* and I survived! Now the real game was on. Any fumble, any miscue would mean the end of the line for Ben-X. There would be no second chance. There was too much at stake on that one shipment for the captain to take any chances with an unwanted and undeclared passenger.

Ben-X made it to the truck that he had picked days in advance. He lifted the heavy, waterproof cover and eased his way inside. The truck was not easily accessible and was away from all traffic. Ben-X had already hidden a few bottles of drinking water, some granola bars, and a bag full of assorted candies. The changes in temperature could be very sudden when traveling on a ship. Ben-X had a sweater in his bag. He chose not to wear it just yet, as he knew there would be plenty of opportunities for him to use it. Overdressing right from the start would be a grave mistake. Ben-X was praying and hoping that his choice of the back of a truck was a good one. With the cover serving as a dome, Ben-X's shelter looked like a small room. He could turn at ease and move his legs freely, not that he wanted to be completely relaxed and careless. That could be very troublesome and could carry extremely serious consequences.

As time went by, Ben-X became very familiar with all the different noises aboard the ship. He could distinguish the footsteps of three different crew members who would walk down the hallway approximately every three and a half hours. Occasionally, two of them would stroll by together and Ben-X would try to listen to their conversation. He gathered that one of the crewmembers' names was Manno and another one was Rene. They started by talking about the weather.

"I could bet you five bucks that it is going to rain in less than two hours," said the first crewmember in a raspy voice.

"Rene," sand the second one, "I don't know about less than two hours; it seems more like the rain will start in the next thirty to forty-five minutes."

"I would still win then," said Rene laughingly.

"This is why I would not bet you," Manno said. The conversation took a more serious tone.

"Do you think the new guy in the Haitian Customs office will be a problem? What is his name?" Rene asked worriedly.

"I don't think so. I don't see how he could have such an important job if Lieutenant Colonel Franklin did not OK him," Manno said reassuringly.

"You're probably right, but those new guys can be a real pain. They sometimes seem so overzealous," Rene continued. "Remember—last time it ended up costing us some of the merchandise."

"What do you care? That is just the cost of doing business. Pass it on to the consumer, as they say," Manno responded.

"I hope you are right," said Rene, still unconvinced.

Rene was relatively new in the business. He used to sell real estate in Orlando, and had been lured into his current profession by his longtime friend Manno, who told him how easy it was to make a few grand each time they had a successful run to Port-au-Prince. Rene could not resist. He was on the verge of financial ruin after his wife had literally taken him to the cleaners following a nasty divorce. He had lost his 200,000 dollar house, while his ex-wife Ghislaine ran off with another man. Life could be so unfair sometimes. Rene knew of the risk that he was taking, but he was hoping that this opportunity would help him get back on his feet quickly.

Manno, on the other hand, seemed much more comfortable in this line of business. He used to be a car dealer. One day he was offered a large sum of money if he would make sure that a particular car would get the necessary documents for leaving the country. A fake invoice here, some backdating there; Manno had passed his initiation into the underworld. He was rewarded with an envelope with 6,000 dollars and had been on the team since. He was completely hooked and could not leave the ring even if he wanted to. He is a very crafty individual and can usually talk his way out of the stickiest situation.

These characters on the boat were of a much different breed than Ben-X. They could not care less about the political implications of their transactions. They could not see that by keeping the supply line to the de facto regime going, they were, in fact, keeping the killing machine fully operative. They could not see the situation beyond their individualistic vantage points. "I bring goods to the regime. I get a large sum of money. I am happy." The cycle resumes again and again. Manno and Rene's conversation continued.

"Do you think," Rene asked, "that the embargo is going to last that long?"

"I have no idea," Manno said. "It is a lot of bull. Do you really think that *Blan Meriken* wants an embargo on Haiti? Can you imagine how much money the Miami port alone is making out of this situation?"

"Are you telling me that the Americans do not want the crisis to be over?" Rene asked, more confused than ever.

"You believe in *Tonton Noel*, Rene. All it would take would be a warplane to land in Port-au-Prince and an ultimatum to the high-ranking officers. 'Hey, fellows, this is the last plane out! If you do not get on it, we cannot guarantee your safety.' Do you remember how Baby Doc left the country?"

"Why put the embargo in place then?" Rene inquired.

"It is only a bluff," Manno countered. "The guys in Haiti can get whatever they want, whenever they want it. Everybody is making money. As for the elected president, by the time they bring him back, he will be a toothless, weak, and transfigured president—a pale photocopy of what he used to be."

"Why bring him back then?"

"Well, they have to make it appear as if they are in support of democracy," said Manno. "This is even a bigger bluff. They spent millions of dollars to lure the masses into the polls and then overthrew the winner, because they did not like the results. Anyway, I don't care one way or another, as long as I can make some money. The embargo can last forever."

Manno and Rene were no political scholars. They were just two commoners who saw an opportunity to jump on the bandwagon and make some profits. They understood something about political alliances, though. They knew that Jean Bernard Alexandre did not stand a chance. He was allowed to rise from the masses only after the bourgeoisie realized that they could not resist and that they needed to respond to the persistent and loud demands of a more and more vocal populace. They quickly surrounded him, and under his shadow, they were able to satisfy their appetites, as Machiavelli would say. The *petit bourgeois* that became part of Jean Bernard Alexandre's camp never intended to articulate the demands of the masses, nor did they understand them. As for Rene and Manno, they represented the ever-growing group of opportunists who were ready to sell their souls for a dollar. If confronted and asked for their positions on any political matters, they would quickly respond that they have none. They subscribed to the economic philosophy of free enterprise—as if there could be such a thing in an economy that depends, for the most part, on humanitarian contributions. Manno and Rene were just tradesmen. They delivered the goods to whoever comes up with the dough. "I don't become involved in politics," was one of Manno's favorite responses whenever his friends would try to engage him in any kind of discussion.

23

As Ben-X listened to the animated conversation between Manno and Rene only yards away, an overwhelming feeling of sadness came over him all of a sudden. The past year and a half of his life had been quite uneventful. At no time had he taken time to deal with his own feelings of loss. He was a man who had lost just about everything: his family, his friends, and his country. At no time had he had the opportunity to shed tears over the death of his mother, Mrs. Lespinasse, and his three beautiful sisters. He had lost the majority of his friends, yet had remained numb throughout the events. All of his energy had been used up to ensure his own survival. Now that he had made the decision to go back home and confront his enemies under his terms, he no longer felt powerless. He would find more strength in acknowledging his own weaknesses and humanity. He had been dealt a horrendous emotional blow and it was perfectly appropriate for him to feel the pain and to be stricken with sadness. Tears flowed down his face like a torrent. He must have been sobbing for some time, when he realized that it could be very dangerous. Fortunately, the sobbing noise was muffled by the continuous deafening sound of the Caterpillar 12 engines. As an added bonus, the rain had started to come down. It was two hours later than both Manno and Rene predicted. Both of them would have lost the bet.

Ben-X was not just crying for the loss of his family members and his friends; he was crying for the degradation of his native land and the hopelessness that he had witnessed in the eyes of thousands of Haitians rescued at sea as they were trying to flee the burning island. It was ironic that these people in distress did not welcome the giant Coast Guard ships that were ready to offer them food, water, and first aid. They knew that it was like the last meal offered to a death-row prisoner about to be executed. They knew it signified the end of their efforts to find freedom. They would end up in captivity and then be returned to the opened jaws of the sharks back home. They would be tossed right back in front of the barrel of the gun of the Haitian strongmen. If they did not end up in mass graves, they would have to thank only Lady Luck for their good fortune.

Now there was a clear sense of purpose to Ben-X's life. His own demise was meaningless. It was true that the military men could catch him and subject him to the most inhumane treatment. They could torture him. They could destroy his physical being fiber by fiber, but no way were they going to get to his spirit. His spirit would live on as a man on a quest for justice and freedom. He would become immortal. Every *sans-logis* on the streets of Port-au-Prince would carry on the fight. His spirit would live on in every one of the *restaveks* sent away out of love by desperate parents who fell for the false promises of better homes, better environments, and better opportunities for their starving children, only to find out that their beloved children had been made into modern-day slaves. His spirit would live on in the slums of Cite Soleil, La Saline, and Bel Air. His spirit would live on in the indomitable revolutionary zeal of the youths in Raboteau who had always stood up to oppression. Maybe Ben-X would fall, but he had become the symbol of a whole nation, which had resisted the relentless attempts of the enemy to vilify her and keep her subjugated. Like a willow, Ben-X might fold and kiss the ground from which he came, but he would spring back with more energy than ever.

Ben-X's tears were like the sacred water that was going to purify him and wash away every bit of uncertainty and insecurity that characterized him and all human beings. He was not ashamed to let all of his anguish out. He knew that after he let all of his tears out, he would be as strong, as firm, and as deadly as a bow in the hands of an Indian chief. There would be no enemies too powerful for him to take on. No roads too arduous, no obstacles too insurmountable. He was ready to face just about anything in his pertinacious pursuit of justice. Fear no more! Insecurity no more! He would be like a fox. He would stalk his enemies around the clock and strike them when they least expected. He would move with the deceptive ways of a ninja. He would run them down until they had no place to hide, nowhere to run. As far as Ben-X was concerned, the hunt had started, and this time he was the hunter. The arena would be the mountains and valleys of his beautiful country. There would be no holds barred. Ben-X would transform into whatever or whomever; he needed to be close to his prey in order to surprise it. Like Ulysses did to the Cyclops, he would strike the enemy right in the eye. His reach would have no limits. He would be a shoeshiner or a *machan fresco.*[1] He would be a porter or a gardener. He would be a beggar or a deliveryman. The ends justified the means.

Since he could not take on his enemies with overwhelming force, he would need to outsmart them. His flexibility and his versatility would be his weapons. He would display the *flair* of a hound, the eyesight of an eagle, the speed and agility of a black stallion. He would move with the speed of lightning and would strike with the strength of a gladiator. He would sleep with one eye closed and would keep a watchful eye on the enemy at all times. Every time his enemies made mistakes, he would be there to exploit them. In the end, victory would belong to him.

The St. Philomene had been at sea for a full day. From Ben-X's standpoint, so far it had been an uneventful journey. He had even ventured out for a few minutes once he was sure that most of the crewmembers were asleep. Surprisingly, the captain did not seem in a hurry to get to Port-au-Prince. Ben-X remembered the engine being shut off completely at least twice. Was there a problem? Whatever it was, Ben-X would never find out, unless, of course, he got lucky again. He was hoping his unwilling informants would walk by and have another discussion again. Or maybe not. The longer they stayed away, the better off he would be.

Ben-X had one essential task to perform as soon as possible. He needed to verify which one of the boxes contained the weapons. He knew for sure that large, olive-green metallic containers had been loaded onto the ship. He could not tell what they contained, but they looked quite suspicious. What could be in those boxes to warrant such precautionary measures? The ship was transporting much more than foodstuffs to an embargoed nation. Ben-X had to be patient.

Note

1. Snow cone vendor.

24

Opportunity would avail itself soon, Ben-X hoped. He knew that there were seven crewmembers on the ship. If he could account at any one time for their whereabouts on the ship, he would be well ahead of the game. The captain and the pilot never really left the upper deck where the command post was located. From what Ben-X could hear, there were at least four of them involved in an animated game of *besigue.* The loser was being mocked, had been forced to cover his face with flour, and was not being very graceful about his misfortune in the game. He accused the winner of cheating. The loud argument could be heard at the other end of the deck. Where was the seventh man? Had Ben-X miscounted the crewmembers, or was the seventh man lying somewhere making up for lost sleep? If he only knew he could go on his little exploratory mission. Ben-X waited for the mantle of darkness to once again cover the ship. "That should be soon," he thought.

From under the giant cover of the truck, Ben-X took a quick peek at the hallways. They were unusually quiet. Not a soul was in sight. Ben-X let himself out of the truck. His legs felt heavy, since he had not used them for hours. He caught himself and moved cautiously. He had looked at this area so many times that he knew every obstacle of the crowded course. He needed to get to the back of the ship to check some of the sacks. He thought he heard some footsteps. He quickly hid behind the supporting pillar. False alarm. No one was in sight. Ben-X pulled out his pocketknife and sprung it open. He jabbed the first sack and found nothing unusual. Then the second one. No problem. A third one. Bingo!

The tip of his knife met a very hard metallic object that almost bent it. Whatever it was, someone thought it was important to conceal. Ben-X wanted to have some of it. He palpated the hard object with that exquisite sense of touch only owned by the blind. He could feel the characteristic elongated shape of rifles. Ben-X's heart was racing. That the St. Philomene was trafficking weapons made Ben-X's presence on the ship even more dangerous. Should he be caught, he probably would receive a bullet in the head and be tossed overboard. No one would even miss him. No one knew that he was on the craft. Ben-X cringed at the thought of being served as dinner to the sharks. He moved the sack around to a spot where he could easily recognize and retrieve it. The most difficult part would be to get it off the boat when the time came.

That was enough exploration for the time being. Ben-X decided to get back to his hiding spot. He dined on a piece of stale bread and a bottle of fruit juice. He had a Mars chocolate bar for dessert. Ben-X smirked at the idea that he might pull the whole operation off after all. To face such a tremendous challenge and succeed would be one hell of an accomplishment. It would be even a greater joy to beat the enemy at his own game.

Ben-X had no idea what the travel plan was. He knew that under normal circumstances, the trip between Miami and Port-an-Prince would have taken a mere seventy-two hours. They were probably more than half-way there. Ben-X was lying in the truck half asleep, when it dawned on him that he had not checked the truck in which he had been hiding. He looked at some well-wrapped boxes in the truck and had no idea what they contained. How could he find out without raising any suspicion? The plastic wrapping was very tight. Ben-X knew that sooner or later his curiosity would get the best of him. It was just a matter of time. He slowly and carefully peeled off the plastic using his pocketknife. The side of the box was now completely exposed. He turned on his flashlight and inspected the box. It read:

Explosives. Handle with care.

Ben-X could not contain his surprise. Now, he really wanted to have a closer look at the contents of the box. Explosive devices with timers, dynamite, hand grenades, and bullets. What was going on? Wake up, Ben-X. There is a war going on and you were not invited. Wow! What a find! All this time, he was lying in the middle of a sea of explosives and did not even know it. Now, he understood the meaning of the signs, *Absolutely No Smoking,* which seemed to be all over. Ben- X had found it quite strange, because he did not think that the crewmembers were all that health conscious. On second thought, maybe they were. Smoking on the ship could instantly spark one of those giant explosions that would certainly cause the death of everyone. "Thank you anyway," Ben-X thought jokingly. "I will remember not to light up my birthday candles."

Ben-X was so preoccupied with his plans on how to get off the ship with some of the goods that he had just discovered that he could not fall asleep. It would not be a good idea to get off the ship and come back. It would be much too risky. He had no idea how quickly the weapons would disappear in the Haitian market. If he could, maybe he could find out the final destination of the weapons and try and get to them at a more fortuitous time. That did not seem like a good idea. There was just too much chaos in the country right now, and Ben-X had no guarantee that Haiti was the final destination of the weapons. There was always the possibility that Haiti was just a stopover in a broader Caribbean arms trade. Now that there were no longer as many leftist revolutions being started all throughout Latin America, the arms manufacturers needed a new market for their merchandise. The neighborhoods in the cities were being transformed into a no-man's-land, with enough firepower to fight a small war. Ben-X had to come up with a plan before long. Whatever the final plan was, he would have to execute it swiftly. No room for mistakes. He needed to seize every single opportunity, because he did not know whether or not there would be any more while he was still on the ship. Ben-X needed to get rid of the rice from the sack he had identified as containing weapons. He did not undo the top of the sack. He made some tattered marks on the sack to simulate rat bites. Ben-X had not had visual confirmation that there were rodents on the ship, but he had come across something that looked and smelled like rat excrement. Ben-X did not think it would be a wise idea to go on a rat patrol at that very moment. He just wanted the crewmembers to believe that they had been had by a herd of rats. *Rat Kay, kap manje pay kay.*[1] His mission was to empty the sack of its grain, in order to make it easier to conceal and transport the weapons off the ship. He made several trips and threw a large quantity of rice grains overboard each time. Ben-X now had further confirmation of the presence of the rifles in the sack. He could not see them, but he could palpate the contour and feel the firmness of the metal through the sisal material around them. What a feeling! Progress was being made.

Every step was bringing him closer to the legitimate and basic right to defend one's self against tyranny and abuse—the right to respond to whoever was continuously slaughtering innocent people. A people whose only dream was to live in peace and to have a voice in the affairs of their country. So much had been asked of them and so little had been given to them in return. They had been betrayed, humiliated, and forced to live like sub-humans. The very people in whom they had placed their trust had come back to hurt them. They had always been very docile. Every day they got up and took care of the business of the city while the rich men were still nursing their stomachs and recuperating from their overindulgence at the previous night's banquet. They never complained about the fact that nobody ever visited them once the elections were over. But yet when there was a conflict between the big shots, they were the first ones to be massacred.

The night after the coup, the armored trucks and the tanks had not been deployed in the rich neighborhoods. If you asked anyone from the upper class about the disruption that the continuous shooting had created, the answer would probably be one of surprise. "What disruption? We never heard a single shot." The time to even the score and put an end to this situation was drawing close. How many of the victims came from the upper class? Only the slums and the overpopulated areas were targeted.

Note

1. "It was an inside job."

25

Ben-X knew that his sojourn on the St. Philomene was coming to an end. He had had more close encounters with other members of the crew. They were not as loquacious as Manno and Rene, but they did indicate that they were expecting to be in Port-au-Prince in less than a day. As Ben-X tried to figure out how he would get off the ship with the weapons, he realized that he needed some rope. He had already gone through the box in the truck and had filled his bag with as many grenades, bombs, and rounds of ammunition that he could carry. The difficult part was going to be the bag containing the weapons. If he could find some rope, maybe he could lower the package in the water and pick it up later. With a bit of luck, he would be able to do this without attracting much attention. It was worth a try.

Ben-X left his hiding place during the last hour of darkness. The early signs of dawn were all around the ship. Everyone was still asleep except the captain. Ben-X remembered seeing a long sisal rope in the utility room with the broom and the bucket. If he could only retrieve it. He moved swiftly and his steps hardly touched the wooden deck. The rope had been moved. He started to panic. He quickly scanned the area. In one of the corners he spotted the rope. Ben-X grabbed it and retreated to his shelter, taking with him the package that contained the weapons. The package now looked completely different. It looked as if the weapons had been wrapped and handed to a wary buyer at a flea market. At least now Ben-X had everything that he needed in one place.

The last and final challenge of his journey would be to escape from the boat without being detected. Ben-X realized that he had not washed or bathed in three days, and was afraid that his body odor would give him away. However, he was hoping that the stench on the boat and the breeze from the Caribbean Sea would mask the pestilence. He did not realize that after a few days of exposure to the stench of the boat, he had started to take on a smell that was neither his nor that of the many items around him. The fear of offending the noses of his unwilling hosts put aside, Ben-X had another challenge ahead of him. How would he get off the boat without being caught? Ben-X had to admit that until now, the events had gone his way. He had survived almost three days on the boat. He had been able to find everything that he wanted and had been able to get some rest. He had no idea what adversities were ahead of him. He seemed to have been waiting for this kind of a challenge all his life. He had been able to do without the little comforts that people so readily took for granted—like taking a long, warm shower at the end of the day, or relaxing in one's favorite recliner to read a book. Ben-X had had no such luck. He had not slept in a bed for days, and his neck and back muscles were feeling the mistreatment they had been through. At that moment Ben-X could have used a good massage and some stretching exercises. Not a chance. Ben-X went into some deep relaxation routines and meditation. He had difficulty clearing his mind. He was much too preoccupied with the unanswered question about how he would get off the boat.

They were fast approaching the bay of Port-au-Prince. Ben-X could just feel it. When he had left the country about eighteen months before, he had been under a lot of duress. He had just created quite a stir, thanks to the miscalculations of Lieutenant Colonel Franklin, who underestimated the degree of repulsion that the populace had toward their oppressors. Oh boy, did the Haitian people have fun. In less than a week, hundreds of Ben-Xs had been sighted all over the country. Ben-X had become a magician who had the gift of ubiquity. Ben-X was here, he was there, and he was everywhere.

That was then. Now the situation was more serious. Ben-X was ready to strike back with a lot of force. He was getting ready to respond to the butchers by using the only language they knew. The *lex talionis*[1] was in order. It would be an eye for an eye . . . For the moment, whatever subterfuge Ben-X was going to use, it would have to be a safe one. He needed to create a diversion, a state of confusion and panic that could give him a cover to leave the boat. What could he possibly use? Fire was out of the question, for it would certainly create a giant explosion given the kind of goods that were being transported on the ship. No one would survive. The crewmembers were big-time smugglers, but they did not deserve to die. Maybe someday they would develop a conscience and money would not seem that important to them. "What is the next best thing to fire?" Ben-X asked himself. "Smoke, maybe? But it is a known adage that there is no smoke without fire. Not exactly," Ben-X thought. "Dry ice! Of course. There must be some dry ice on this ship." Meat and poultry were shipped to Haiti in very large amounts. There were even some rumors about handguns being transported inside frozen turkeys. "There must be a large freezer on this ship, but where was it?"

Ben-X imagined that he had about an hour or so to find out, or it would be too late. Should he take a chance of venturing outside the truck this late in the trip, and risk everything? The prospect of falling into the hands of the military men in Haiti was even worse. If he was going to get caught, it might as well be before they reach the port. He could always invent some cockamamie story about sleeping on the boat and finding out too late that the boat had taken to the seas. Would they buy it? Maybe not. On the other hand, if he could find the necessary material to create a diversion that would allow him to escape, his chances would increase a hundredfold.

Ben-X decided that it was worth the risk. He walked around the ship, his eyes scanning everything. There it was: a large metallic container, the kind you see on the highway being pulled by large trucks. Inside the container, large cuts of beef, pork, and poultry . . . and, most important, plenty of dry ice. When the moment came, Ben-X would have to get back in there and carry out as much of the cold stuff that he could. The timing would have to be perfect. He would have to be close enough to the shore to be able to swim away, but far enough to escape detection by onlookers who always seemed to be in the wrong place. Hopefully that large basin of water at the other end of the boat would still be there. Ben-X had a plan. It would have to work. There could not be any mistakes.

The boat became less noisy all of a sudden. They were still moving, but the speed of the ship was reduced to a bare minimum. Through a rip in the cover over his hiding place, Ben-X peeped outside. He could clearly distinguish the landscape of Port-au-Prince, which sat there like a wounded dog waiting for the early morning sun to shed light on its multiple sores. Here and there lay neglected neighborhoods, human waste, stagnant water, flies, and pestilence. A place that used to be a city had fallen into decrepitude. No matter how repulsive Port-au-Prince looked, it always inspired that special feeling that is experienced only by the native who is coming back to that place called home. It had been the longest period of time that Ben-X had been away from his native country. His last trip had been more than six years before. It had taken him to the bateys of the Dominican Republic, where Haitians were basically enslaved and forced to work under inhumane conditions, while officials from the Haitian government made huge profits. Lured by promises of decent work in the sugarcane plantations, thousands of Haitians had been recruited and forced to work long hours—sometimes with no sleeping quarters and very little to eat. Ben-X had felt obligated to make the trip to help the workers organize to demand an end to the situation. They did manage to draw the attention of some of the international human rights organizations. However, the Dominican officials had retaliated by summarily returning Haitians who were legally established in the country. Ben-X had received many death threats, but that did not deter him from completing his mission. He remembered coming back home to find his country still in turmoil.

This time Ben-X did not know what to expect. His sources within the country had indicated that the killings had not stopped. Haiti was still a country under the gun. Families were still being terrorized. Teenage girls and young mothers were still being violated. Many stories were still waiting to be told. Stories about the horror of a regime that wanted, at all cost, to keep its grip on a battered country. More important, stories about the resistance of a people unwilling to succumb. The Haitian people had resisted foreign enemies with prowess, and now they were being forced to resist enemies from within. For the past two years, the stories had been transmitted via *telediol* and had been like the serum of life running through the veins of a people unwilling to die. The pain and the anguish of the population seemed unbearable, yet the Haitian people would not accept defeat. Instead, they seemed to have decided that there would be no more tears. Bodies were being tossed on the streets of Port-au-Prince every night in plain view of anyone willing to look, as if the people needed to be reminded of who held the guns. There would be no more tears when yet another raid on the slums was reported in grand fanfare. A furtive look of disgust on his face, the passerby would cover his nose and then would move on. When passing a pile of garbage on a street corner, if one is pusillanimous, one might proceed with caution, for there might be some human remains sticking out. There were no tears left in the eyes of the elderly woman who had earned the nickname, "the hibiscus lady." For almost two years she had gone around town every morning covering the faces of the dead and placing a small bouquet of freshly picked hibiscus by each one of them. Rumor has it that she lost her mind following the death of her only son immediately after the coup. Well into the night, you could hear her yelling with her raspy voice, "Sergo! Sergo!" It has been almost three years and no one has been able to convince her tht her Sergo will not be coming back. Sergo is gone forever. Call her deranged; call her whatever you wish. She is a hopeful sign that humanity refused to die. The spirit of the Haitian people had refused to die.

The ship had drawn awfully close to the final docking place. Ben-X needed to act right away or else it would be too late. Soon the deck would be filled with officials and businessmen happy to see that the "Embargobuster" had defied the patrolling ships of the U.S. Coast Guard. There would be large sums of money changing hands. The captain of the ship and his crew would be thousands of dollars richer. The Haitian Army and its supporters would keep the killing machines going for another few weeks until they ran low on supplies again. The St. Philomene was just one of a large fleet of cargo ships that was making a fortune out of the misery of the Haitian people. The official line was that the embargo was an affront to the sovereignty of the poor nation. Behind the scenes, the smugglers were applauding the situation. Never had a poor nation created so many millionaires overnight. Ben-X was realistic about his chances of pulling apart such a well-organized and well-equipped machine, but he certainly was going to try everything in his power to slow it down. Whatever little victory he could claim for his people would be very welcome.

He was an excellent swimmer who could easily make it to the shore should he decide to get off the ship at that time. He looked around. The hallways were completely deserted. Very soon there would be a lot of agitation. Ben-X went straight to the freezer and retrieved as much dry ice that he could carry in a plastic bag. He then quickly moved to the other end of the boat and tossed the ice into the basin. Smoke filled the ship. Ben-X had all of his belongings securely attached to his back. He retreated back behind the truck and waited. He did not want to run the risk of coming face to face with some crewmember. He counted all seven crewmembers running to the front of the ship, where the visibility was reduced to near zero. There was panic on the ship as the smoke spread all over.

"We had better control this fire quickly, or the whole boat is going to explode!" shouted one of the crew. The captain rushed in with a fire extinguisher in his hands. There was total panic on board. It was the moment that Ben-X had been waiting for. Like a fox, he quietly lowered himself down in the lukewarm Caribbean water. The water was very invigorating. Ben-X could feel a jolt of energy going through his whole body. The water was not the cleanest, but it mattered very little to Ben-X. He could take it anytime. Ben-X had returned home. He could not claim that he had returned into friendly territory, but he could at least say that he was where he belonged. It was his birthright. He was 100 percent Haitian. He knew that it did not make any difference whether his persecutors were American Immigration officers or overzealous thugs who happened to be Haitian. He was ready to give them a run for their money.

Catch me if you can!
Catch me if you can!
I have the speed and agility of a cheetah in the African bush.
I have the strength and the grace of a black stallion.
Catch me if you can!
I have a huge wingspan and I can descend on you with
the precision and the stealth of a bold eagle.
Catch me if you can!
I can be as noisy and scary as a laughing hyena
and as nimble as a black ninja.
Catch me if you can!
I have the eyesight of an owl
and can see you through the night.
Catch me if you can!
I can be your gardener in the morning
and your strangler by day's end.
Catch me if you can!
I will be Joe. I will be Robert.
I will be Timothe. I will be Pierre.
I will be Marie-Carmel. I will be Irma.
I will be Linda. I will be Julieta.
Catch me if you can!
My name is Ben-X and I have come back to hunt you.
I will be your worst nightmare . . .
A thorn in your side until you say uncle.
Your days of joyful and free rides in the swamp are about over.
God save your souls.

Note

1. Talion's Law.

26

Ben-X swam underwater for a good two minutes before he came up for air. The ship was still cruising . . . going around in circles. Ben-X was out of danger. He went back underwater, swimming directly toward the shore. The more he could look like any usual swimmer, the better off he would be. It would certainly look very suspicious if the luggage he was carrying with him could be detected. He managed to attach his duffel bag and the package containing the rifle in one big bundle held together by the rope. Swimming was more difficult, but still manageable. The distance that he had to cover was not too long. He was now well within the area where some swimmers sometimes venture when they wanted to show off their athletic skills. He wanted to have a good idea of how crowded the beach was. As much as he wanted to touch the soil again after having hurriedly escaped the country close to eighteen months before, he knew that timing would be his best ally.

He would have to find a hiding place for his weapons. The best place would be one that was easily accessible before and after each operation. His plan was to land on an isolated section of the beach. When Ben-X got off the ship, he had faced a very populated section of the southern end of Port-au-Prince. If he could reach the shore in that area he could easily get lost in the crowd. He knew the area perfectly well, as it was not too far from Fontamara, where his family had been massacred. Not that he had any intention of finding out what had happened to the property that technically belonged to him, since he was the sole heir to the Lespinasse estate. Maybe sometime in the future. For now, there was more important and pressing business to attend to.

Ben-X had been in the water for almost an hour. He was scanning the area, trying to study the landmarks. He could clearly distinguish the small restaurant/bar where he had dined a few times. The place was renowned for its conch *Creole* with fried plantains and rice and beans. Ben-X was feeling hungry just thinking about the delicious dish. He wondered what happened to Suzanne. He used to be physically attracted to that woman. She probably had a large family with children running all over the place by now. Ben-X was surprised at his own physical shape. For now, he was just another Haitian swimming in Haitian waters. He was far enough away from the ship for anyone to suspect that *that* was why he was swimming with his clothes on.

Ben-X realized that he needed to take care of this odd scenario. He took off his clothes and held on to them, being careful not to lose them to the current which was getting stronger as the day was drawing to an end. The sun was getting ready to set. The darkness was going to be Ben-X's best ally. He had every right to be where he was, although he had often stated tongue-in-cheek that his little portion of the Haitian land had long been claimed by foreigners. Deep in his heart, he knew that he could rightfully claim, "I am not an alien." How could anyone have any doubt? The first Haitian Constitution had granted Haitian nationality to all people of African origin who had chosen Haiti as their country. Ben-X was more than eligible. Ben-X was Haitian . . . very Haitian . . . 100 percent Haitian. Let there be no mistake about it. It had been exactly 535 days since he left home incognito. He had returned home the same way that he had left: incognito. It was only appropriate for him to do so. If he could walk into a law office and file a lawsuit against all of the people who had done him wrong, maybe he could take his mask off. His country was not ready. Therefore, he would remain undercover until further notice. This time, however, he had a very deliberate mission.

Ben-X had been in the warm tropical waters for a good while now. He could have reached the beach if he wanted to, but he was waiting to approach the beach at the most fortuitous time. Staying in the water too long would start raising suspicion. The hours after the beachgoers abandoned their beach homes would be the perfect time. He would have plenty of time to scout the area for a hiding place for his precious load. As he took his last strokes to reach the beautiful white sand of Bizoton, he was greeted by the most memorable sunset. The sun was descending slowly behind the horizon in an explosion of colors. The crimson color of the sun had tinted the whole Caribbean sky and was reverberating over the still waters of the sea as if through a kaleidoscope. Only minutes ago, the same water had different shades of blue. The sea was like a priestess who had adorned her most sumptuous vestments for a celebration that was about to begin. The day was making a desperate and futile effort to last a few more moments. Not a chance. The night descended suddenly over the region, enveloping it into a giant drape. Was there any reason why the sky had the color of blood? Any reason why the sky was on fire? Were the gods transforming the night sky into a giant sponge that would suck up the blood of all the innocent men, women, and children that had been spilled unnecessarily? The night was queen, and no one could predict what mystery or what new tragedy she would bring to the troubled island.

Ben-X could not contain his enchantment. Heavy-hearted, he kissed the ground for the third time. For eighteen months, he had been kept away from his beloved country. He had been chased and persecuted like a common criminal. If wanting every Haitian to be treated with dignity was a crime, to this crime Ben-X pleaded guilty. If desiring justice for all the fallen heroes of this brutal but undeclared war was a crime, to that crime, too, Ben-X pleaded guilty. If, on the other hand, it is a crime to keep a whole country with a gun to its head . . . if it is a crime to twist the law of the land . . . to violate the Constitution . . . then Ben-X wanted to shout without ambiguity, "I hereby find YOU guilty, guilty, guilty!"

All around town, men and women fought against the obscurity by lighting candles, putting together pine torches, and lighting kerosene lamps. If they were lucky, they would turn on their light switches. Their attempts would be to no avail because nothing and no one can fight off darkness on this land . . . unless, of course, your name is Ben-X. Ben-X has returned to push darkness back. He has come to put some balance into the game. He is well aware that he cannot even the score. There have been thousands of victims on one side already. But he could stop the killers right in their tracks. At least, the game would not be a shutout.

Part Five

Inside the Lion's Den

Si vis pacem, para bellum.
(If you want peace, prepare for war.)

—Flavius Vegetius Renatus
(Instit. rei milit, III, Prol.)
Treatise of Military Act

27

David shouted in reply, "You come to me with sword, spear, and javelin, but I come in the name of the Lord Almighty—the God of the armies of Israel, whom you have defiled."

—David kills Goliath, Samuel 17:45

Ben-X was quite happy about being back in his native land. He had had quite a journey so far. He had been close to death many a time, and had always managed to get away. As he expected, the small houses were deserted at this time of the evening. The owners had gone back to their homes inland and might not return for another day or two. He would probably be undisturbed long enough to perform his delicate task.

He needed to find a good hiding place for his weapons. He found an empty wooden box and some rags in one of the houses. He carefully wrapped his automatic rifles, his bombs, his grenades, and his ammunition and placed them in the box. He used a stick to dig a hole in the ground. The soil was fairly soft and presented no difficulty. Some seawater crabs ran away from the scene, as they felt intruded upon by this unusual visitor. Ben-X dug the hole deep enough to contain the box without raising any suspicion to the area. He would need to be able to find the place very easily. The worst thing that could happen was that he might have to change location. Everything would depend on where he chose as his general area of residence.

What would his next move be? Ben-X could not help but think that most developed nations had long adopted the position that their enemies should be dealt with by using overwhelming force. They had embraced with great enthusiasm the philosophy of Machiavelli: "It is better to be feared than to be loved." Countries like America and the United Kingdom could go to war in a matter of minutes. As a result, they had enjoyed long periods of relative peace. In the case of Haiti, for most of its history, the enemies had not come from outside the borders, but from within. Haiti's true enemies had not been some foreign nations that would start hostilities with Haiti. They had been the Haitians, themselves. There have been more Haitians killed at the hands of Haitians than at the hands of all other enemies combined. The imperialist nations had been able to infringe on the sovereignty of Haiti only with the complicity of Haitians. Haiti's true enemies were Haitians. If there were a war to be waged, it would have to be against Haiti's enemy from within. It is the duty of every true patriot to identify the enemies and bring them out in the open. Those people who, in the middle of the night, had conspired to bring death and desolation to the Haitian families were the true enemies of peace. They were the true enemies of Haiti.

28

Day 600

The situation of the Haitian people is desperate. The killing has become more subtle. Efforts were made to clear the streets very quickly of the dismembered bodies of the opposition to the de facto military regime. Sometimes, however, there were just too many bodies. The morgue stopped receiving cadavers. Some youths have disappeared. Rumor has it that the victims were taken out to sea and dumped in the water with heavy weights tied around their legs. Bands of thugs roamed the streets, terrorizing peaceful citizens. Respectable women were humiliated. Wives were violated under the watchful eyes of their husbands. The whole country has sunk into chaos.

The strongmen in Haiti are emboldened by the inaction of the opposition. The international community has been talking tough, but has done little to displace the regime. The opposition is divided on the practicality of an embargo. Every time the regime seems to bow under pressure, relief is offered. The Haitian people have no faith in the international community to put an end to its slow death. The Haitian people are feeling betrayed . . . abandoned. They are ready to play the refugee card. The de facto regime no longer feels that it has to sit at the negotiating table. The parliament has mastered the art of dilatory speech making. There seems to be a legal justification for every illegal act that the unlawful regime poses.

Day 601

Pirate Radio Broadcast from Somewhere within Dominican Republic

"Haitian people, do not be discouraged. Operation 'Fe koupe fe'[1] is about to start." Simultaneously, in an unprecedented act of defiance, small planes loaded with pamphlets from the opposition to the military regime fly over several major cities and litter the streets with messages from the deposed leader. Finally, the Haitian people are thinking. It is about time! Somebody, please help! Sadly, the only effects the leaflets have are to give more excuses to the bloodthirsty attachés to kill more innocent citizens. Anyone caught with the leaflet in his hands was beaten, sometimes to death. Some were simply shot. Ben-X needed to give an appropriate response to the latest rash of repressive acts.

Day 602

Ben-X had been monitoring his first target for many days now. The resistance movement, even though it did not engage in violent acts of retaliation, did do an excellent job of collecting intelligence information about its enemies. A whole network of fax transmissions linked people from all around the world. For example, Ben-X knew, well before landing on the shores of Bizoton, that the Carbaret military post was listed amongst the locations where a lot of abusive incidents were taking place. It was a real house of horror. Carbaret was under the command of a captain nicknamed *Pataswel*.[2] He enjoyed slapping his prisoners on both temples at the same time, causing his victims to lose their hearing or fall unconscious to the ground in their own blood.

His victims had, at times, defecated on themselves and had been made to clean the floor with their bare hands, if not their mouths. That such atrocities were allowed to continue at the dawn of the third millennium is unimaginable. Such reprehensible acts do not just tell about barbaric Haitians; they tell about the whole human race. Wherever they are committed, they must be denounced and stopped. Villagers were regularly taken into the military complex and submitted to long hours of torture. The screams could be heard at a distance well into the night. When the torture chamber was in session, the whole town knew about it.

Ben-X did not have any trouble gathering some tactical support for what he was about to do. The house of horror had to go. He was very careful not to let anyone know too much about his plan. The less his supporters knew, the less exposed they would be, and the safer it would be for them. Soon after his arrival in Haiti, he moved to Carbaret and lived among the people, putting the final touches on a plan that he had rehearsed over and over in his head.

Notes

1. "Steel cut steel!"—meaning, armed resistance.
2. A slap.

29

Ben-X was pleasantly surprised that the enemies he faced were very unsophisticated and had no idea how hated they were in the small town. They had left their flank wide open. Like most armies in Third-World countries, they saw the civilians around them as servants to take care of all of their needs. They depended on the civilian population for food, laundry, and sexual favors. That would be their Achilles tendon. Ben-X also took notice that large containers of gasoline were being stored on the grounds of the small military complex. The commander of the post obviously wanted a share of the black market. Well, Ben-X was going to seize the opportunity and capitalize on this practice that stood in defiance of common sense.

The mood at the military post was particularly festive that night. The menu included *tasso cabrit,*[1] fried plantains, and rice and beans with a sauce of *piment ti zwazo*.[2] Some of the officers were drinking large amounts of Rum Barbancourt; others were consuming *zo devan* and *tafia,* which were 150-proof alcoholic beverages. No one knew what the occasion for the celebration was. When an army officer felt that he was in total control and that he had a whole country at his feet, when he knew he could have any girl in the town to attend to his sexual needs, why did he have to have a reason for celebration? By 8:00 P.M. almost everyone in the station was at least half-drunk.

For good measure, the servant had added large doses of Valium to the soldiers' drinks. Guess who was serving the food? A very elegant woman in her mid-forties, dressed in a long skirt and a colorful top. Her eyes were accentuated by a touch of mascara. A very discrete layer of lipstick completed the makeup. She wore a neck-length wig of a carefully chosen shade that matched her skin tone. A blue printed headband made her look quite dashing. Some element of grace and dignity was emanating from that woman. One of the half-drunk soldiers could not take his eyes off her. It made the lady quite nervous. "This man had better cool it, and not have any ideas," she thought. The lady was there on a very specific mission and was not going to blow her cover over some sweaty, half-drunk military man with a strong body odor.

The food must have been particularly good that night. The small group had had several servings and the lady was left with very few leftovers. Little did they know that they needed to savor every bit of that delicious meal, because it might be their last. The military personnel were not the targets of this particular strike, but there was a strong possibility that they might become corollary casualties. It was remarkable how much help one could find in a town in which every inhabitant was fed up with the abuse of army officers who acted like a hostile occupying force. They would arrest young men and women, beat them up, and threaten to kill them unless their families could come up with some large sum of money for their releases.

In the matter of the people of Carbaret versus the army of coup makers and putschists: "We the people of Carbaret . . . find you guilty of kidnapping and false imprisonment. We the people of Carbaret find you guilty of rape. We the people of Carbaret find you guilty of extreme cruelty. We the people of Carbaret find you guilty of crimes against humanity. You are guilty of extortion. You are guilty of perjury. You are guilty, guilty, guilty . . . "

These military men had taken an oath to protect the

nation. Instead, they were putting the Haitian people through a slow and painful death. It was just a matter of time before the Carbaret people demanded that a punishment be carried out. The time had come. The lady, after serving the food, went in the back to the outdoor water spigot to wash the utensils. No one paid attention to her. The soldiers in the small cafeteria had just finished their dinners. Some were slouching on the army issued furniture. Some of them were trying to figure out how to steal each other's money at a game of poker. They were all completely drunk. They could not have lifted a finger, should they have come under attack. The combination of Valium and alcohol had had the desired effect. They had no idea that their drinks had been laced.

The lady quickly entered the storage room where the containers of gasoline were kept. She pulled a small bomb made of dynamite sticks and a digital timer out of her bag. She placed it in between the barrels of gasoline. The red numbers read 15:00 and started to count down. "I'm outa here," said the lady. She left as easily as she came in, walking through the front door. There, she left a red kerchief with a red penny with an "X" marked across the dead president's effigy. She also left a leaflet with a message that read:

> No longer will you be allowed to roam free in this country and maim, torture, and kill with impunity. So whenever you are about to maim, torture, or kill another innocent Haitian, Remember Carbaret! Remember that maybe you are next!
>
> Ben-X

In order to make sure that the Haitian Army did not squash the message, arrangements had been made for the same leaflet to be faxed to different places around the country. Gone were the wig and the long skirt. Gone was the makeup. The master of disguise was back to his old tricks. Welcome back home, Ben-X.

Ben-X was miles away when the usually quiet area was awakened by the sound of a small explosion followed by a much louder one. That night, there was no need for electricity. The huge fire that lasted for hours lit the sky. The military post was burned to the ground. The house of horror had all but disappeared. The only structure left standing was the gate with the handkerchief still attached to it. Had the soldiers gotten away? No one had stayed behind to take count. If they had, how could they have explained to their commanding officers in Port-au-Prince that they had been drunk while on their post? Their greed and eagerness to get rich quick on the local population's misery had given Ben-X a golden opportunity. If one looks closely enough, the enemy's mistakes can easily be discovered. The enemy always furnishes the Gordian knot with which to strangle himself. There was not supposed to be any gasoline on the premises.

When the armored trucks and tanks rolled in the next morning, full of mean-looking soldiers in fatigue uniforms, all they found were some stray cats and dogs that looked like they had been abandoned by their owners. They, too, were casualties of the ongoing hostilities. The inhabitants of the small town had taken to the hills minutes before the explosion. They seemed to have been tipped off as to what was reserved for their torturers. It was not just coincidence that the incident occurred on a night when most of the inhabitants were out in the neighboring town of Arcahaie. Carbaret had become a ghost town overnight. The Haitian people had a long tradition of *marronage*.[3] During slavery time, they would hide in the mountains when the situation became unbearable. They would wait until the situation cooled down and would return with even more determination. The battalion that came into town was both angry and wary. Most of the soldiers would have preferred a different assignment. If the rumors they were hearing were true, there was a strong possibility that they might be shot at. It was never supposed to happen that way . . . that someone would actually attack an army post. That person must have had a whole band of armed people behind him.

Carbaret was no place to hang out. Attempts were made to cover up the incident. The rulers certainly did not want the population to get the feeling that they were losing their grip on the situation. Not a chance. The leaflets with Ben-X's signature were being photocopied and distributed all over the country. The news of his return spread like a brush fire. Freshly painted signs were springing up on every empty wall. The resistance movement had received a new lease on life. Finally, there was hope that the enemies of the people were going to get a run for their money. Finally, there was at least a faint possibility that the soldiers, who had acted so boldly and so arrogantly when they were the only ones holding the guns, might be scared. The army barracks at Carbaret did not exist anymore. The target had been acquired. The thugs would have to find another location to torture the people of Carbaret.

The local papers would not dare to report about Carbaret. The radio stations were tight-lipped about the event. Yet, the more the authorities tried to squash the news, the more rumors and innuendoes were allowed to fester. By the time the news got to the other main cities, these rumors had become gargantuan. There were stories about a man who could sneak in on soldiers like a ninja and inflict fatal blows. The diaspora papers made a media frenzy out of the incident. The headline from *L'Observateur* read:

Haiti on the Verge of Civil Warfare

The paper went on to discuss how a disorganized opposition is determined to gain back power at all costs, even if it means plunging the country into a civil war. It went on to discuss the impact that a civil war would have on the life of the Haitian people. At no time did it comment on the suffering and the grief of the people. The undeclared war against the Haitian people did not bother *L'Observateur.*

The more radical and avant-garde newspapers put it in a different perspective. The weekly newspaper, *La Marche,* wrote:

Ben-X Propones Talion's Law: An Eye for an Eye,
a Tooth for a Tooth

Actually, it did not matter what the newspapers said. The point was that the operation in Carbaret had refocused the attention of the world on the plight of the Haitian people. Maybe the killings would slow down. The citizenry would get a breather. In that sense, the operation was a resounding success. Unfortunately, it also meant that Ben-X had to be extremely vigilant. There was going to be an all-out effort to capture him.

Ben-X was ready to handle the pressure. He had made a conscious decision right from the start that his own life was far less important than the survival of a whole country. There was no greater honor than to die for one's country. Ben-X could not help but think about the words of "The Dessalinienne":

Pour le drapeau, pour la patrie,
Mourir est beau, Mourir est beau

Notre passe nous crie
Ayez l'ame aguerrie
Mourir est beau, Mourir est beau
Pour le drapeau, pour la patrie.

For the flag, for the country,
To die is beautiful, to die is beautiful
Our past yells to us
Be mentally ready
To die is beautiful, to die is beautiful.

Ben-X did not have a death wish. As a warrior and a freedom fighter, he was well aware that death awaited him at every corner and at every turn in the long and arduous struggle for justice and equality. Maybe one day, the country would find peace again. Maybe one day, Haitians would respect the life of other Haitians. There would be a renewed covenant among all Haitians to live in accordance with the country's motto, *L'union fait la Force.* Then, Haitians would be able to live as brothers without the fear of being stabbed in the back, without the fear of betrayal. Maybe then, all Haitians would be able to enjoy the splendor of the land. What a celebration it would be. There would be dancing in the streets. There would be *fetes champetres*[4] and carnivals all over the country. The Haitian spirit, the spirit of bravery that had guided the Haitians through popular uprisings against slavery, would be regained and Haiti would shine again. Haiti would sit amongst the nations as an equal among peers, not out of pity. Nothing would be in the way of Haiti's economic development. It would be a country where respect for the law and for the rights of others would be the bread that gives sustenance to every Haitian. Arts and music would flourish like never before. Everything would be back in order.

Meanwhile, there was much work to be done. The various political factions could not agree on how to get the country out of a crisis that had been created by greed, pride, and obstinacy. Like puppets, the protagonists were playing right into the hands of those who could not care less whether Haiti continued to exist as a nation. It caused Ben-X great pain to watch his country fall into a state of stagnation. While the leaders made long speeches about nationalism, they were selling the country away in exchange for fat bank accounts abroad. It was not that the corporations were necessarily out to steal coins out of the beggar's hat. The majority of them wanted a sound and fair business deal that was likely to last and bring profits for all parties involved. Most of the time, the foreigners walked away with exceptionally advantageous deals. But because the Haitian leaders were eager to get their kickbacks or were not shrewd enough to negotiate good deals for the country, they would end up giving the store away. It was quite shameful that a country with such a glorious past had become the laughingstock of the other nations. The pain had to stop. Ben-X was going to be part of the solution.

Notes

1. A goat entree.
2. Very spicy.
3. Taking to the hills to escape persecution.
4. Rural festivals.

30

Day 615, Downtown Gonaives, Haiti

The popular groups decided to organize a demonstration to protest the recent decision of the de facto government to increase the price of gasoline, flour, and rice. The heads of the household were finding it increasingly difficult to feed their families. The authorities who seized the opportunity to increase their profit margins were feeling the bite of the embargo. More than 1,000 people took to the streets, braving the near ninety-degree heat. They were told that no demonstrations were allowed, but they defied the ban. People who could be identified as supporters of the de facto regime had infiltrated the crowd. Supporters of the coup were seen hoisting signs demanding the immediate and unconditional return of the deposed president . . . in order to put him on trial. It was a setup for disaster. What was supposed to have been a peaceful march degenerated into a brawl between the two factions. Bottles, rocks, and other missiles were thrown. Blood was all over the streets. Shots were fired. There were dozens of wounded and one dead.

An army platoon under orders from (guess who?) Captain Marcelus started to shoot into the air. A stray bullet hit a pregnant woman, who fell to the ground. Lacrimogen gas grenades were tossed into the crowd. More panic. A group of youngsters decided to run to the sea toward a fishing boat where they had been hiding. They were trying to swim toward the fishing boat. The soldiers chased them with their automatic weapons blazing. The youngsters did not stand a chance. In less than fifteen minutes all the shooting had stopped. The corpses of seventeen young boys and girls lay floating in the water. Some of the bodies were still on the sand. Some of the youngsters had been hit at least seven times. It was yet another massacre in the same city in which, a few years before, the death of two school-age youngsters had triggered the final push leading to the downfall of the Duvalier dynasty.

This time, the blood was all over the hands of Captain Marcelus—the man who had been the main author of the massacre of Ben-X's family almost two years before. How many more deaths had this man caused in between the two massacres? How many more cold-blooded murders would he be allowed to commit before someone stopped him? Would it not be justice if someone put a halt to this man's actions? How many lives would be saved by this man's death? In an organized society, this man would be arrested, charged, put on trial, and found guilty of multiple murders. He would have to serve a just sentence. How would such a scenario happen in a lawless society? Who enforced the rules against the military man who could single-handedly decide that a whole family was guilty for having a different political point of view, and put the family to death instantly with no questions asked? Who would dare say no? Who would dare stand up to the gunmen who were butchering the Haitian people? When had anyone brought to justice renowned perpetrators of crimes against the Haitian people?

Never. It had been the same story over and over again. The headlines in the newspapers could have easily read, "The rapacious bird that got away." Not this time. There was no system in place ready to deal with the large volume of cases that no one had the intention of bringing before a nonexistent judicial system. Captain Marcelus had willfully and intentionally caused the deaths of at least several dozens of peaceable and innocent citizens without any consideration for their surviving family members. Many lives would be saved if Captain Marcelus' insatiable thirst for blood could be stopped. "I, Ben-X, the jury, hereby find Captain Marcelus guilty on all counts. He must no longer be allowed to maim, torture, and kill innocent citizens of this country. He is found guilty of crimes against humanity. He is the enemy of the people of Haiti. He is the enemy of Haiti. He is hereby sentenced to death."

For many months, even before Ben-X came back to Haiti, he had already accumulated a large amount of information on Captain Marcelus. He knew, for example, that the captain had fallen into disgrace and had been transferred to Gonaives following what was described as the debacle of Fontamara, during which Ronald St. Fort had escaped capture. Gonaives was to be his testing ground before he received any promotions. Captain Marcelus had something to prove, and had become an overzealous and vicious killer who was very trigger-happy. His men had been instructed in the following terms: "If you are having any trouble with a group of troublemakers, shoot them all." The Gonaives assignment was particularly important, since any serious trouble was likely to come from this town that had a long tradition of rebellion. Ben-X also had learned that Captain Marcelus and Lieutenant Colonel Franklin had quarreled over a beautiful brunette by the name of Melanie. For many months, Captain Marcelus was not seen in public, as he was afraid that the lieutenant colonel might carry out a threat to have him shot. According to Ben-X's sources, Melanie chose Marcelus over

Franklin. The lieutenant colonel was heartbroken.

Melanie and Marcelus had been sighted at their hiding place on Grosse Roche Beach. They went there every Friday afternoon, when they could have the white sands all to themselves, away from the eyes of the curious. Or so they thought. Captain Marcelus had been under surveillance by the resistance movement for almost a year. His movement patterns, the cigarette brand that he smoked, his favorite drinks were all carefully noted. Ben-X knew that Captain Marcelus liked Hennesey on the rocks and that he would get into a very good mood if offered a large bottle of the expensive cognac. On Fridays, Marcelus liked to cruise around in an old convertible Wrangler jeep—one of three vehicles he owned. He usually left an Uzi on the back seat of his jeep and traveled without any bodyguards. He was just another Haitian Army officer struck with the common virus of invulnerability. He was stuck at the level of an adolescent and sincerely believed he was invincible. The profile of this officer would prove to be invaluable when Ben-X was ready to deal him a deadly blow.

31

The porch of the Gonaives Cathedrale had a new inhabitant. An old man with dark glasses and graying hair could be seen there. He carried a staff in his right hand. His left hand was wrapped up in dirty, old rags. Ben-X was at it again. He spent time in front of the *cathedrale* every day, begging for money in a soft and unassertive voice. In fact, he was more interested in collecting information than in collecting the few *gourdes* that he would receive from the rich people of the town. The interaction was usually very awkward. The well-dressed churchgoers would give him uneasy and furtive looks, as if they were afraid they would be magically struck with a curse from a genie. They looked as if they were afraid to be suddenly changed into frogs for interacting too long with a beggar.

A good beggar can usually get very close to anyone. He is often adopted by some institution where he becomes part of the decor. When a new beggar invades a territory, the current beggars, to see if he is legitimate, often put him through some test. The new, blind beggar introduced himself as Compe Manno to the senior beggar, Ti George, and they began a conversation.

"I have been doing this for many years now. Life is not what it used to be," Ti George started.

"I know what you mean. What I collect at the end of the day cannot even buy a good meal," responded Compe Manno.

"Do these people know that I have children to send to school and a wife, just like them? They probably don't.

Everyone wants to act as if we don't exist. We are sores in the eyes of society," lamented Compe Manno. "We remind everyone, every day that there must be a better way."

"You are right about that," Ti George agreed. "The people who drive these *Tet Boeuf* do not see anything wrong with things the way they are. Try to say anything about it, and you are dead."

"Not everyone is the same, though. That captain seems like a cool guy, doesn't he?" asked Compe Manno.

"Captain Marcelus?"

"Yeah!"

"You must be crazy! All he does is kill people and run after women. He must have at least three mistresses in this town alone. Do you know what he does with common thieves?"

"What does he do?"

"When they do not share the loot with him, he has them shot in the cemetery at night. They shot two last night. You can go to the cemetery and look for yourself."

"You know, Ti George, I have heard people say this before. I just thought they were making it up. You know how they are always making up stories about officers. I even heard that some would have their prisoners perform sodomy while they drank and watched," remarked Compe Manno. "I guess, like any other large institution, the army has all kinds of people—including perverts. This Captain Marcelus, he is a womanizer just like many others."

"Oh, no! They say that when he is at home, his wife runs the show. Everybody in town knows about his escapade with Melanie," replied Ti George.

"I have heard that one, too."

Indirectly, Compe Manno (Ben-X) had obtained all the

information that he needed for then. It would be just a matter of time until he stalked his prey and found the opportune time to finish him off.

32

Ben-X started hanging out by the main road, watching the passing cars. He noted that every Friday at about 9:00 P.M., an olive-green jeep would slowly drive by with an athletic-looking man sitting at the wheel. It was unmistakably Captain Marcelus. Ben-X obtained further confirmation one morning when he observed him entering the military barracks in full military garb on Avenue Toussaint Louverture. Everyone had stood at attention as the captain made his grand entry. No doubt that the sun was about to set on this killer's life. His card was about to be pulled by the specter of death. Soon the innocent people of Gonaives would breathe easy.

Day 627

9:15 P.M.: Route National No. 1, near Gonaives

It was a beautiful night. A half-moon was watching over the town. The day had been extremely hot and a fine rain had just brought the temperature down a bit. Ben-X was dressed in black and was wearing a mask over his head. This time the operation would have an added measure of danger. After completing his strike, he would take advantage of the darkness of the night to disappear into the woods. He had studied the area very well and was confident that the operation would be successful.

Ben-X waited by the roadside, hiding behind a mango tree. He was sweating profusely as he waited for his prey. He had carefully placed a log and a dead goat in the middle of the road, thereby forcing any driver to slow down a bit. Ben-X had been waiting for almost half an hour when he heard the very distinctive noise of the jeep engine. He took a deep breath. As the jeep approached the log it almost came to a sudden stop. The driver had not noticed the obstacle in time. It was the moment that Ben-X was waiting for. Like David tossing his rock at the head of Goliath, Ben-X disarmed a grenade and tossed it into the jeep. A loud explosion rocked the night. The surprise was total. The jeep blew into pieces. The wheels flew in all directions. A mass killer had just been terminated. The target had been acquired. All around the scene of the explosion, leaflets were spread, along with a red handkerchief with a penny tied up in one corner. Across the effigy was a red "X." The leaflets read:

> Too long had this killer been allowed to kill innocent people. This one is for the Lespinasse family who were savagely killed in Fontamara on September 30, 1991, and for all the innocent victims of Marcelus' insatiable thirst for blood. Anyone willing to follow his example shall have the same fate.
>
> Ben-X

With his duffel bag tossed across his shoulder, Ben-X disappeared into the woods like a shadow. He was one with the darkness of the night. It would be morning before anyone realized what had happened. By that time, he would be miles away. The army would judge it ill-advised to venture into the darkness of the streets of Gonaives less than a week after the massacre on the beach. The investigation regarding the loud explosion would have to wait. Remember the words of Manno Charlemagne:

Nimpot ti bwi tankou Latoti
Yo kouri kache.[1]

The response from Ben-X had been proportionate in the misdeeds of Marcelus—a man who felt that he could kill without any fear of reprisal. How many children had become orphans because of this man? How many wives had become widows because of this man? Tyranny had been allowed to last too long because of this man. Remember the words of Jean-Jacques Rousseau: "The first slaves were made so by force; the state of slavery was perpetuated by cowardice." Tyrants cannot be allowed to take over a country's life and push the people's faces in the mud without resistance. It is a sacred and inalienable right of every human being to defend himself when his life and humanity are threatened. In the troubled nation of Haiti, the citizens had been terrorized. Every bit of dignity had been taken out of their lives. That situation needed to be stopped at all cost. When a city can no longer police its citizens, when the criminals are the very ones in charge of fighting crime, a state of chaos settles in. The society becomes decadent and is condemned to fall apart and disappear. Eliminating Captain Marcelus and others like him was not stopping the process, but it certainly was slowing it down. There was no doubt that the world would be better without him. For now at least, the people of Gonaives could breathe freely. Their torturer had been terminated. The people of Gonaives could sing:

La rose fe banda
Toutan soley pa leve.

Nan jadin mwin gin you ti fle yo rele libete.
Chak fwa yo rache-l li pouse anko.
Libete, libete, libete . . .
*(Grenn Banbou, Radio Asoto)**

Morning dew princes around, only before the sun rises.
In my garden, there is a little flower called freedom.
Any time they pull it out, it grows back.
Freedom, freedom, freedom . . .
(Grenn Banbou, Radio Asoto)

Yeah! In their hearts, the people of Gonaives were singing and dancing that morning. Although there could not be any outward display of joy (that could be deadly), there was a discreet smile on the face of everyone. To each other, they whispered the words, "Ben-X strikes again! Long live Ben-X."

Note

1. "At the least noise, they run and hide."

* Used by permission from Jean-Baptiste Obas.

33

Everyone at the military barracks was stunned. The people in uniform obviously did not share the joy of the population. They were mourning the death of their boss. They could not believe that anyone would have the audacity to perform such an act. The military men were obviously discounting the degree of anger and rage that the population was experiencing. The army had totally lost touch with the people. Ironically, for the first time, the commissioned officers had something in common with the enlisted personnel, the *Ti soldas*. They were sharing a very common human feeling. A feeling that was so prevalent in the hearts of the entire Haitian population for over two years was now theirs, too. Fear. It was written all over the faces of everyone in the military unit. What made it worse was the uncertainty and the mystery surrounding the enemy they were facing. Who was the enemy? Were they under attack by a large-scale armed resistance? Did they really want an answer to these questions? If they only knew that every Haitian had become their enemy because they had stepped over the line. They had taken hope out of the hearts of the Haitian children. They had lowered the status of Haiti in the eyes of other nations. Now their worst enemy was their own fear.

Panic had taken over the barracks. Lieutenant Altemar, the deputy commander, had assumed interim command of the post. He looked like he had not slept in days. He had already smoked at least two packs of *Comme il faut* since being abruptly awakened from his bed at 1:00 A.M. by the *officier du jour* with the news of a huge explosion off the main road. At first they did not know how serious the situation was. There were rumors that the captain had escaped unscathed. That would have been a miracle, given the force of the explosion. Parts of the captain's body were found many feet away from the site of impact. Lieutenant Altemar did not quite know how to react. It was both an opportunity and a grueling challenge. Assuming the command of the unit in a time of crisis was not Lieutenant Altemar's idea of a promotion. In fact, he was quite happy with his position as the second man. He was included in every deal and got a cut of any major business, yet he assumed no responsibility for any screwups. He just cruised along and never got blamed when something went wrong. Now he had to rise to the occasion and possibly send his men to face a popular uprising. Yeah, popular uprising! This was the kind of drama that was taking place in the barracks that morning. Such a possibility was always taught at the *Academie Militaire,* but no one really believed that it could happen. When was the last time the Haitian Army faced real, unfriendly forces?

The heat was on and Lieutenant Altemar's stomach was letting him know. He had made several trips to the unsanitary bathroom already. The military men were finally earning their salaries this time. The enlisted men were extremely nervous. The love of their families suddenly took on immense importance. What if they were sent in harm's way and did not get to see their loved ones again? They wished they could just drop their uniforms and their rifles and run home. The ones who had been caught off duty were very hesitant to report to the military barracks. They were under a lot of pressure from their wives not to show up.

"Why should you go and fight the war of the big shots

of the army? Look, you cannot even feed your family!" said the wife of an enlisted man. The army unit was in complete disarray. Fear and lack of commitment can be a very destabilizing combination for an army that finds itself suddenly without a leader. For the first time, the prospect of losing their lives for a cause that they had not embraced hit the enlisted soldiers. If the all-powerful Captain Marcelus could lose his life, what about them, real peons situated at the very bottom of the ladder?

The Gonaives army unit did not know what to make of the new incident. A communiqué was transmitted to the Army Headquarters in Port-au-Prince. It was hard to say whether the officers really believed that the sky was about to fall on them, or if they wanted to make sure that the Port-au-Prince unit was going to come to their rescue. The following encoded communiqué was sent over the military radio:

> Situation very unclear at this time. Captain Marcelus has been assassinated. We are taking all measures to capture the author(s) of this terrorist act. We will need additional units. Population still on edge after the incident on the beach about a week ago. Please advise.

34

This time, the army leaders did not send a whole battalion to pacify the area, as they had done in the past for situations of this gravity. Rumor had it that Captain Marcelus' nemesis, Lieutenant Colonel Franklin, had not shed a tear and even had had a bit of celebration. Someone had done what he had wanted to do, himself. It did not matter to the general public. Some sector of the population still believed that the whole story was a hoax masterminded by the army to get rid of its own enemies from within—those who might stand in the way of the lucrative drug business. Maybe that is why the reaction from the army was so unusually muted. No massive arrests, no raids in the slums of Raboteau. The local population could not stand another series of arrests or killings, anyway.

The streets of Gonaives were unusually quiet in the days following the hit on the Route Nationale. Captain Marcelus' body was transported to Port-au-Prince, where he was given a state funeral and commensurated with his rank in the Armed Forces of Haiti. As for the investigation, an official communiqué was read over the media. It ended with the usual *L'enquête se poursuit.*[1] It was the official end of a man who had caused much grief to many Haitian families. *Que la terre lui soit légère!*[2]

In the eyes of the army, Ben-X was a terrorist, an *apatride,* a renegade who needed to be stopped at all cost. At least that was the official version. However, the army did not seem to have the political will to go after him; nor did they seem to have the skills to do so. Maybe the reason behind this uncharacteristic lackluster response was because the incidents could not have come at a worse possible time. The strategy of the army was to lay low in order to give to the world the impression that things were returning to normal—that a return to constitutionality was both unnecessary and risky. The army was courting the ever-intrusive and interfering American ambassador. When the new *nonce apostolique*[3] presented his letter of creances from the Vatican, the event was widely publicized and touted as a sign that the de facto regime was about to be recognized by the outside world. The regime also needed to negate the recent report by Amnesty International describing Haiti as one of the places with the most abuses, where human rights were violated at least once very hour. If they were to go after Ben-X, they needed to do it very discreetly.

The army once again had misjudged the genius of the people, who had a much different take on the situation. As far as the Haitian people were concerned, Ben-X was doing the people's work. His actions were putting some kind of balance into the picture. Every youth wanted to be a Ben-X, and, in fact, they were all Ben-Xs. Each time they refused to cooperate with the army, they were Ben-Xs. Each time they resisted the temptation to give out information about their neighborhood leaders in exchange for a few dollars, they were Ben-Xs. Every day they woke up with the determination to resist oppression in whatever shape or form. To fight oppression from black masters and white masters, as Nelson Mandela so eloquently prescribed, would be their goal.

The people knew that Ben-X was their man. They had no idea who he was. All they knew was that they needed to protect him from the predatory hands of the coup makers. It was an extraordinary task, since they did not know where he might show up next. Well, you could always count on the Haitian people to show resourcefulness in times of crisis.

That had been the trademark of a nation that was always on the verge of extinction, but yet had always managed to survive.

What did the Haitian people do to protect their man? They started reporting sightings of him everywhere. Overnight, Ben-X had become this mythical figure with supernatural powers. He got his power from the same god that had once visited Boukman about 200 years before at the ceremony of Bois-Caiman, when the slaves revolted against their masters. Only such a spirit could confer the kind of abilities that Ben-X was believed to have. Ben-X became that invincible man who could be several places at once. He could take on any man in one-to-one combat. He was an explosives expert. He could infiltrate any place. He could be a priest among the priests. He could be a soldier amongst the soldiers. He could change into anything that he wanted.

The living conditions of the Haitian people were deteriorating daily. The people needed a hero, so they created one that would give them hope and fulfill their own fantasies of vanquishing their powerful enemy. To prove their hero's existence, a series of small activities performed mostly to annoy the enemy started happening. Leaflets appeared everywhere, announcing newer and bolder attacks on the army. Smoke bombs and other suspicious packages showed up in military buildings. The tables were turned. The Haitian people were engaged in full-scale psychological warfare against the de facto government. They had the power of numbers. The army was out-manned and outsmarted. A well-organized campaign of civil disobedience was under way. The people stopped paying their utility bills.

The Haitian people had become ungovernable. The pressure started to show on the faces of the soldiers. The braggadocio talk of earlier times was gone. Every man was out to save his own skin. Gone was the *esprit de corps* often used to describe the army. Many incidents of insubordination were reported. Enlisted men were deserting by the dozens. Soldiers were no longer following orders from their commanding officers. A state of anarchy within the ranks was fast approaching. For a moment, it seemed like the army was going to collapse.

Notes

1. "The investigation continues."
2. "Let the earth be light on him."
3. Vatican ambassador.

35

The de facto regime and its allies were feeling very frustrated over the stubbornness of the people and the show of public support by some Latin American and European countries for the deposed government. They needed to do something drastic, so they decided to submit the Haitian people to abuses like never before. An organization composed of misfits and *caracteres louches*[1] came to life. It was called KAMPE (Konbit Ayisien pou Mache Pran Enemi).[2] The members of KAMPE were not necessarily Duvalierists, themselves, but they were the children of Duvalierists *de la premiere heure.* Until then, they had been mere speechmakers who longed for the nostalgia of the Duvalier years. They would gather and drink while rehashing old stories about how the Duvaliers had created prosperity and built roads, airports, and government buildings in the country. Presently, they wanted to do more than just reminisce. They wanted to protect the country from foreigners. They wanted to keep the country of Dessalines from being soiled by the "stinky feet of foreigners." To carry out what they believed to be their duty, they would use sticks, knives, automatic weapons, and grenades. They would use whatever means their powerful allies would put at their disposal. They would intimidate their opponents into submission, or they would bury them dead or alive. They meant business and they were going to prove it. The rhetoric was back, but did they really believe that a country like Haiti could survive in complete isolation and out of the realm of international law? Or were they just bluffing? The latter seemed more accurate, for it was believed that they were being financed by another branch of the same government whose official policy was to return Haiti to constitutional order.

Was the United States thinking about constitutional order without the deposed president? At times, it sounded and looked as if that was exactly what it meant. The statements and the behavior of the American ambassador in Port-au-Prince contradicted official statements out of the Oval Office in Washington. Whatever the KAMPE members were supposed to do, it was doubtful that part of the scenario was to humiliate and embarrass the almighty American Armed Forces. A group of not more than fifty individuals, armed with batons, machetes, and some obsolete rifles, prevented a missile-armed nuclear powered Navy ship from performing its official duty—to unload several peacekeeping officers in Port-au-Prince. Was it gamesmanship, or was it that the occupants of the ship were afraid of the spirits that the warriors on the dock claimed they were possessed with? Whatever the reason, it would have to be a double entry—both in the history and the comedy books. It was truly a bizarre turn of events! Someone had failed to do his homework into the background of the freshly recruited CIA operatives. They were just opportunists out to make a quick buck, and they were ready to take it from anyone.

The incident shook the confidence of the Haitians being held hostage by the people who were supposed to have rescued them. Additionally, U.S. intelligence picked up a conversation between the head of KAMPE and one of its members, in which they discussed plans to kill an American official visiting the country. Apparently KAMPE wanted to gain some credibility. The effort would have to be extraordinary to be worthy of the trust of a disillusioned people. For the first time, serious talks about a possible armed intervention in Haiti to restore order started to surface. KAMPE members were everywhere. Bold, brash, and unleashed, they hesitated in front of no one. They were operating in the words of a foreign diplomat, like a band of *voyous*.[3] They seemed to enjoy their reputation . . . the scarier, the better. Perhaps their enemies would just melt at their sight. They invaded the airwaves and the written media. They seemed to be everywhere, and were opening headquarters all over the country and even in major North American cities. They were represented wherever there was a large concentration of Haitians. *"Vive la democracie!"* American taypayers' money was being used to promote hatred.

The rise of KAMPE was considered by many a strategic move by the original authors of the coup. The excesses and ultranationalist positions of the gun-toting, saber-brandishing, and flag-waving group had one goal: to make the more moderate right-wing members of the putschists more palatable. This move was remindful of the re-appearance of the Duvalier ex-interior minister on the political scene a couple of years prior. His appearance was to make the Washington candidate, the ex-minister of finances under Duvalier, more acceptable to a timorous Haitian people desperate to see an end to several years of instability. The Haitian people didn't buy it then, and it was not going to work this time around, either. A putschist by any other name remains a putschist. The Haitian people were not going to be fooled. The CIA would have to come up with a more intelligent plan.

The tactics used by the ghoulish group were borrowed right out of the pre-Christian era. How could they commit such atrocities against their fellow citizens, and yet claim to be fighting for Haiti's advancement and progress? It was completely insane. Remember the words of Jeanne Manon Roland, as her head was about to fall under the guillotine: "O freedom, what crimes are committed in thy name!" The revolutionary fervor of a group of zealots was destroying humanity one day at a time on that little speck on the planet named Haiti. Every human being had the moral responsibility and duty to oppose it, denounce it, and fight it. Where was the press of the civilized world when families were being systematically terrorized? The Haitian people felt betrayed and abandoned. There were no special reports—no outcry from the free world. The Haitian people felt as if they were facing slow death alone. The houses of people identified as opposing the regime were marked with red paint, to be hit later with rounds of bullets. People who had lived through the worst of the Duvalier regime would quickly tell you that the atmosphere created by this out-of-control group was far more horrific. In the face of such brutal attacks from the right-wing organization, the Haitian people felt violated. They had nothing to hang on to. The number of bodies littering the streets started to increase again. No one imagined that the situation could get worse, but it did. What are you supposed to do when you find yourself on the ground, mortally wounded, with the enemy still charging at you? There is nowhere to run. There is no escape. If you happen to escape the country on a flimsy boat, you stand almost no chance of making it alive. If, by the grace of God, you happen to make it, you are told that you are not a political refugee. "There is no massive and systematic persecution going on in your homeland," the refugees had been informed.

Still, the ingenuity of the Haitian people seemed limitless. In fact, it was a golden opportunity for the Haitian people to show off their skills. All over the country, people could be observed crushing glass bottles. There was a plan afoot to throw the glass dust in the eyes of anyone identified as a member of the death squad organization. Members of the resistance would climb trees and find way to force the intended targets to look up. When the person looked up, glass dust would be thrown in his face to blind him. One might say the plan was somewhat naïve, but it did not matter. It simply proved that the masses were not about to quit. It proved that when a human being feels concerned, he would resort to the most basic animalistic instincts in an attempt to survive.

There were many other plans to fight off the new wave of KAMPE fascism. The death squad organization was just another nail in the coffin of a quickly decomposing society. It was supposed to have dealt a fatal blow to the resistance. Peace and tranquility had been absent from Haitian life for a long time, and there was no hope of them reappearing any time soon. The growth of the children had been stunted. The Haitian families were in danger of annihilation. It seemed that the plan was to completely exterminate the Haitians as a people. It was quite painful to watch a population constantly on the move. It was even more distressing that Haitians, themselves, were being used to perform this most disgraceful and sordid job. The opposition to the de facto regime was to be brought to its knees and reduced to complete silence

Something needed to be done quickly, or Haiti would simply cease to exist. Signs of desperation were everywhere. Families started to separate along political lines. Husbands and wives found themselves on different sides of political issues. The days of paranoia were back. Fathers could no longer trust their own children. Brothers and sisters could no longer communicate freely with each other. The safety of many militants was endangered. The members of the resistance, who had joined the movement without any political convictions, were the first ones to get discouraged and switch to the other side. The consequences could be deadly, as the situation was handled in the usual manner. The traitors were intimidated into keeping their silence. How long would this strategy work? The resistance movement was hoping that luck would be on their side. Members of the resistance started to show up in very suspicious places. The situation could not be more serious. The death squad organization needed to be struck with overwhelming force. If the inner workings of the organization could be studied and exposed, maybe it would slow down the rhetoric that was now saturating the airwaves. One could not turn on a radio without hearing some kind of propaganda. The virtues of Duvalierism were being extolled. Under the "Father of the Nation," as they liked to refer to Papa Doc, no foreigner would dare insult Haitians. No diplomat would dare call Haitians "bande de voyous." The diplomat would find himself a *persona non grata* in no time. The public demonstrations multiplied. The names, *Dessalines* and *Toussaint Louverture* were used ad nauseam.

In the midst of all this, somehow the resistance movement got a small break. Thanks to the intelligence work of a member of the diaspora, it was discovered that the leader of the death squad organization was on the CIA payroll. At any other time this piece of information would have been discarded as insignificant. Most of the high-ranking officers of the army were rumored to be CIA operatives. This time, the opposition was going to make the most out of this little gift from heaven. The information was played over and over on the news. The leader of the death squad organization suddenly lost whatever little bit of credibility he had. There was dissension in the ranks of the organization. The leader started to show some signs of nervousness. To regain his grip on the organization, he started to make a series of public statements. One morning he appeared dressed like a general from the early nineteenth century. His antiquated costume was complete, and even included the pointed hat and sash across his shoulder, worn only by the forefathers. On his right pectoral area, there were at least five medals. The leader of the organization was a very decorated man. But how had he earned all of these honors? The medals were from his father, who had been the commander of the Haitian Army. Maybe he was a traveler from a time machine. If you had any doubt that this man was from another time, his remarks would have convinced you. He stood in the shadow of the status of Jean-Jacques Dessalines at the *Place des Heros de L'independence* and made the following statement: "The enemy of the country would have you believe that I am working for the CIA. *Jamais, jamais je ne trahirai la nation.* (Never, never would I betray the nation.) I call on all Haitians to unite behind me to protect the soil of Dessalines from all its enemies."

His words did not come out clearly, as he was stuttering very badly. The people in the first line of the audience were sprayed with spit bullets at the rate of three a second. It was a scene out of a comedy movie. It was difficult to figure out what the leader intended to achieve with this masquerade. It backfired. As the leader's discombobulated remarks were shown on the small screen, the children were having a lot of fun. They started to make jokes and mocked him.

Maybe the organization was starting to feel the impact of its lack of popularity. It was a very hated organization. The members planned to start an all-out campaign to spread fear in the population. For no apparent reason, and without provocation, peaceful citizens going about their daily routines were picked up, taken to the organization headquarters, and beaten up with sticks covered with pointed nails. The reason? Who said one was needed? Maybe for just belonging to the masses. Maybe for continuing to hope that, by some kind of divine intervention, their deposed president would come back.

The deposed president seemed to believe it, anyway. When a reporter pointedly asked him, "Presidan Alexandre, eske wap tounin?" (President Alexandre, are you going to return?), he declared, "Yes, I will return, because my name is Jean Bernard Alexandre." He showed a lot of confidence, considering all the evidence to the contrary. Maybe sometimes such statements were needed, especially when the masses were so desperate. However, it was left often to different interpretations. Had the president meant that he was ready to make any compromise to make his prediction a reality? Meanwhile, in Haiti, the terror continued. Hardly a day passed without reports of more beatings, more kidnappings, and more disappearances. The population seemed to be holding on to life by a thread.

Notes

1. Shady characters.
2. Haitian Association to Assault all Enemies.
3. Delinquents.

36

Day 667

Death threats, anyone? If you were anyone of importance, if you were a VIP, or if you were just about anyone who was not in agreement with the political masquerade put in motion by the de facto regime, you were likely to receive a death threat. The warnings took many forms. A motorcycle might slow down by your car window and a strange character would indicate with a finger moving under his neck that you would soon be killed. A note might be stuck by your window, stating that they knew where you were. The warning might take a more gruesome turn—like a well-wrapped, dead rooster delivered to your doorstep. For the majority of the people targeted by such a crass campaign of terror, it did not go any further. However, for the Kadashi family, originally from Lebanon, the threats would be carried out in a very tragic and dramatic way.

The day had started as usual for Gesner Kadashi, the younger of the two brothers. He had just opened his store and was on his way to complete some errands a few blocks away. He did not notice that a red utility vehicle was following him. The car passed him three times, and then gunshots rang out. Gesner Kadashi was hit several times. He fell to the ground. He did not say a word. The merchants ran for cover. No one even thought about coming to the wounded man's rescue. For hours, the unfortunate man lay in his own blood. No police. No rescue. No ambulance. Who could you call when the suspected perpetrators were in charge of the city? Where could you take a seriously wounded man in a country with no trauma center? If you happen to have a heart attack, you are on your own. If you are involved in a serious car accident, you are on your own. If you are seriously injured, the ambulance might get there, but don't count on it.

When a distraught brother came to the scene, Gesner had absolutely no chance of survival. Arnold Kadashi felt absolutely powerless as he watched his beloved brother gasping for his last breath. Why did Gesner have to die like a stray animal on the street? Was it a case of mistaken identity, as some were saying? Had Gesner died because of the political affiliation of his brother? Unlike his brother Arnold, Gesner had not been involved in politics.

After the death of his brother, Arnold was not the same person. He was guilt-ridden. He no longer saw any purpose in life. However, he felt that he had no choice but to continue to fight for what he strongly believed in. In support of the theory of mistaken identity, only days after he buried his brother, Arnold started to receive death threats again. Arnold did not waver in his support of the deposed president and his determination to expose the truth of the intrigues and the conspiracy behind the coup. He did not mince his criticism of what he called the "modern-day pirates" who were selling the country to drug dealers and international smugglers in collusion with the CIA. He did not miss any opportunity to express his contempt for his fellow businessmen, who at no time took into consideration the plight of the poor when they were ready to wheel and deal. Arnold clearly indicated that he had no intention of leaving the country. His struggle would continue. He owed it to the memory of his late brother. He owed it to himself. They could threaten him all they wanted. He refused to live like a prisoner in his own country. He was accused by his grieving friends and family members of being temerarious and "stubborn as a donkey."

Arnold was arrested and detained, but he emerged with a long beard, more determined than ever. He even created a new organization with the sole purpose of spreading the truth. As a sign of his resolve, he started a campaign designed to bring back news coverage of the deposed president. He started plastering the picture of Jean Bernard Alexandre all over town. This was considered by many as one provocative act too many. Some even called it a suicidal wish. It was quite a daring act in a country where murders were committed in bright daylight. At no point did Arnold consider resorting to violence. Many believed that Arnold had the means to hire a mercenary army—if not to clean up the town, at least to ensure his own security. Arnold continued to nourish the utopian hope that the enemies of democracy would come to their senses and that justice would eventually prevail. He placed his faith in God. He believed that the forces of good would prevail over the forces of evil. How could anyone still believe that there was any goodness, any humanity left in a person who could kill, maim, and torture innocent people? How could he believe that words could bring down a completely corrupt system in which guns and bullets ruled? To what court of justice would the evidence be presented? Were there any judges left in town who would dare weigh the evidence he had collected and render justice? Arnold's approach seemed doomed from the start.

Day 711

11:00 A.M.: Eglise du Sacre-Coeur de Turgeau

A group of priests, together with Arnold, had decided to celebrate a mass to commemorate the anniversary of a very lugubrious moment in the recent history of Haiti. They were commemorating the day when a church had been burned to the ground and many people had been massacred with bullets, machetes, and ice picks. The deposed president, who had been the celebrant of the mass, escaped by the grace of God. On that morning at the Church of Sacre-Coeur, the atmosphere seemed very tense. There had been threats. The small audience decided it was then or never. They could not let a group of killers force them into silence. They could not let the killers keep them from celebrating their faith in a God of love and forgiveness. If they had kept silent, they would have had to remain silent forever thereafter. The ceremony began.

Suddenly a group of men dressed in civilian clothes burst into the church, Uzis in hand and vicious expressions on their faces. *"Kote Arnold?"* (Where is Arnold?)

"Here he is," said another voice. Arnold was forcibly pulled out of his pew. The stunned audience could not utter a word of protest. He was made to go on his knees and forced to beg for mercy. He would not. He was shot in the head at close range. What a horrific act! Everyone in downtown Port-au-Prince had tears in their eyes that morning. Arnold had always been kind to all the retail merchants. He had always loaned money to whoever needed it. Now, he was dead.

The sanctity of the church had been violated. Indignity in the troubled nation had taken a mammoth leap. Haiti would never be the same again after that Saturday morning. What would this country have to do to expiate its sins? Would the land forever be cursed? Could Haiti handle the ire of God? Would the wrath of God forever pursue such a degraded land? How far was the death squad organization willing to go?

The horrendous act of barbarism drew a very loud

reaction from around the world. The media once again focused on the situation in Haiti. The inevitability of armed intervention and possible occupation of the small sovereign nation had become apparent. Haiti was critically ill, and the hope of recovery was very dim. Once again, the Haitian intelligentsia remained completely silent. There was no protest from whatever moral forces were left in the country. There had been a blatant violation of the church in a country that was predominantly Catholic, and all that came from the church authorities was a feeble statement. No words were spoken from the Vatican, which was the only foreign state conducting official business with the *de facto* regime.

37

It has been more than two and a half months since the execution of Captain Marcelus. The effort to catch the person(s) responsible for his death had died down. The army's calendar was much too busy. It could not possibly keep up with an investigation that was unlikely to yield any results, anyway. Those kinds of investigations never did. *L'enquète se poursuit*.[1] Ben-X, after having spent weeks in the northern part of the country among the peasants, had moved back to Port-au-Prince more than a month prior to the incident at the church of Turgeau. He had rented a studio in Fontamara under an assumed name but hardly spent any time there. The Lespinasse residence, the scene of his family's massacre, had been condemned. Maybe people were afraid to live there. He was tempted to go there to bring closure to his feelings of grief about his loss, but could not gather enough courage to do it. It was still an open sore that would take a very long time to heal.

The news of the death of Arnold hit Ben-X like a Mack truck. He was livid. It was a tremendous loss. He had had the opportunity to meet Arnold several times. Arnold was a very intense, straightforward, and righteous person. Ben-X was stunned at the audacity of the act. He could not believe that the death squad organization would hit in such an open way. Ben-X learned that the whole operation was allegedly planned and conceived at the death squad organization headquarters. This organization had to be stopped, or else every remaining respectable citizen of Haitian society was a potential victim. Fascism would take hold in Haiti for many generations to come if it was not stopped. The strength of the enemy was formidable, but Ben-X no longer felt that he had a choice. The struggle had to continue until the war was won. Ben-X could not stand to remain passive while the country was being put to a slow and painful death.

The death squad organization had perpetrated, with arrogance, a countless number of crimes against the Haitian people. The world had watched as the ranks of the orphan children grew. Wives had become widows. Mothers had run out of tears. The anguish of the Haitian families was beyond description. The perpetrators were roaming the streets free. Something was wrong. Something was terribly wrong. The Haitian people were begging for relief and demanding justice. When would the court be in session? When would the charges be brought? Let the evidence show that thousands of people had been tortured, killed, terrorized, and kidnapped. Let the evidence show that the Haitian people had been dehumanized. Let the evidence show that hundreds of thousands of people had been displaced, uprooted, and chased from their homes. Let the evidence show that irreparable psychological damage had been done to the Haitian people, and that the seeds of a long cycle of violence and self-destruction had been planted in the Haitian society. Let the evidence show that physical and psychological genocide had been committed. The plaintiff rests.

"I, Ben-X, the jury, in the matter of the Haitian people versus KAMPE, hereby find you guilty on all counts. You are also found guilty of crimes against humanity. The world will be a better world, and millions of people will breathe more freely, when you cease to exist."

Note

1. "The case is still open" is a common and proverbial way that incompetent investigative authorities have used to end their statements in reference to important criminal cases. It had come to signify to the critiques the incompetence of the authorities.

38

Day 750, DSO Headquarters, Delmas 33

KAMPE was actively recruiting new members. It had been emboldened by the apparent lack of political muscle on the part of the opposition. KAMPE and the army were expecting urban guerilla warfare and a popular uprising, but they did not materialize. There had been a few incidents. A couple of KAMPE members had been caught red-handed and were chased by an angry crowd. They were badly beaten and would have perished under the proverbial Pe Lebrun, were it not for a frantic call for reinforcements by the local authorities. Of course, the police were very quick to respond, because this time some of their own were in trouble. They suffered a few casualties. Over all, they could rightfully say that they were fully in command of the situation. For now, at least, they could claim victory. They were winning the undeclared war. They were getting close to celebrating their second anniversary since having taken power. No trouble was foreseen on the horizon. The deposed president had traveled around the globe, but had not set foot in Haiti. He had accumulated awards and honorary degrees from renowned universities for his heroic courage and his tenacious fight to bring democracy back to the island.

In fact, the only true winners were the puppet masters. The de facto regime in Haiti was still in need of its Uzis and batons to rule. The deposed president was slowly but surely being transformed into a figurehead, a very poor image of the feisty leader who had raised the masses to their feet during his Sunday sermons. Like it or not, the puppet masters were the clear winners. From the army's perspective, everyone was aware that it was in full control of the situation. Large sums of money had changed hands. Poorly paid army officers were transformed into successful millionaires in a matter of weeks. Life was good. There was insecurity on the streets of Port-au-Prince. What insecurity? It was a perfect atmosphere for fortunes to be made. A booming business in food products was in full force. Jump on the bandwagon! Become a supporter of the illegal government. You could become rich. It was a government of opportunity for anyone who could keep his mouth shut and look the other way when the killing and the atrocities took place.

There was an official embargo in place. Well, long live the embargo! The longer it lasted, the more money the coup makers and supporters would make. Little did they know that they had been tricked into portraying themselves as an extremist organization whose excesses could be seen as the primary reason for making the country a new form of protectorate. The organization that was pitching itself as xenophobic was negotiating away the right of the sovereign island to its own self-determination. The stage was being set for foreign intervention. In spite of the public posturing, the real deal was being made backstage.

At the KAMPE headquarters, an important meeting was taking place. They were planning a series of demonstrations to demand that the international community keep their hands off Haiti. Signs with very inflammatory messages had been printed. They read:

> Blan Meriken, Remember Charlemagne Peralte
> Koupe tet, boule kay[1]

The second saying was an order given by Jean-Jacques Dessalines after the independence of Haiti in 1804. It was often used whenever Haitians wanted to express anti-foreigner sentiments.

There was a new member in the audience at the KAMPE headquarters. He was a man in his mid-forties with long sideburns and a poorly kept mustache, wearing bifocal glasses. He had the appearance of a math teacher. He participated minimally in the conversation and said just enough not to raise any suspicions. His name was Pradel. He was questioned by one of the recruiters. He told the recruiter a fictitious story about his faith in Duvalierism and how he was happy that an organization was standing up for the progress and the advancement of all Haitians. He gave a spiel about his hope that the organization would become a household name that would rally everyone under the leadership of Brutus, whose father had had a reputation of putting his life on the line for the common good. Somebody should have given Pradel a sip of water to cool him down! He went on and on. Did the recruiter buy it? Of course. Why not? Who in their right mind would not want to join the crusade, the historical movement that would bring prosperity and freedom to the silent majority? Pradel was singing their song, and his speech was very moving and patriotic. Pradel was just being a good Haitian.

It had been a very risky move, but one that Pradel felt he had to make. He was accepted into the organization with open arms. He received a few patriotic accolades and some handshakes. He was in. Pradel wondered how long he would have to withstand this foolishness before he could accomplish his mission. Yes, his mission. Make no mistake about it; Pradel was a man on a mission. He had one goal, and he would fulfill it come rain, hail, or fire. He was fully committed to carrying out the work of the people . . . to carrying out the sentence now pending on the head of KAMPE.

His blow would have to be swift and decisive. Ruin and destruction would be the fate of KAMPE. Ben-X imagined that if he could slow down the organization for a few days, there would be some relief, however small, to the misery of the Haitian population. The degree of disturbance and annoyance caused by the bandit organization was so high that anything that could be done to stop its members would be welcome.

The danger that Ben-X faced was beyond description. Any *faux pas* would, without doubt, bring immediate death. It was as if he were swimming in the middle of shark-infested waters. Ben-X had to calculate his every move. He would be careful not to give away any hint about his true identity. He had to remind himself constantly that he was Pradel, and that he needed to respond to that name in the most natural way possible. He even got a fake identification card in front of the *Bureaux des Contibutions.* It was relatively easy. There were people with stamped forms operating mobile offices with all the blank forms that you could ever want. You could get birth certificates, marriage certificates, and even your own death certificate for a price.

Officially, Ben-X was Pradel, at least for the next couple of weeks. He had set a deadline to accomplish his most delicate mission. September 30. He wanted to have some less painful memories associated with the date. What is good for the goose is good for the gander. The date would also be the people's date. It would be the day the people fought back and won. Once his mission was completed, it did not matter what happened next. A very powerful statement would have been made. If you keep beating a dog, it is likely that one day it'll turn on you and bite your hands off.

The Haitian people had suffered enough, and the time of reckoning had come for the death squad organization. They were going to pay—big-time. David was about to have one more chance at the all-powerful Goliath. Ben-X could hear the cheering crowd. "Go, David, Go! Go, Ben-X, go! This one is for Gesner and Arnold. Let justice be done now."

For all the unclaimed bodies
Because the survivors were too afraid
Let there be justice!
For all the mangled bodies
That no one could recognize
Let there be justice!
For all the crying children
Too young to understand
Where their fathers have gone
Let there be justice!
For all the ones chased away
Who perished at sea
And never reached the promised land
Let there be justice!
For all of those who powerlessly
Watched their country being sold
Let there be justice!

Ben-X had to exercise a lot of control not to jump at the throat of Roger, a KAMPE member who would insult, humiliate, and mistreat peaceful citizens just for staring too long at the headquarters. What was the poor man supposed to do, bow and pray? Ben-X witnessed even more indignities. As the D-day was approaching, Ben-X felt a sense of relief. He did not know how long his nerves could take such abuse without intervening. He knew, however, that he could not let the enemy trick him into a battle that he was not ready to face. He would face it at his time, in his ring, with his rules. He had no intention of losing this battle. Much too much was at stake. He would have to win, no matter what. Should fate decide otherwise, he was ready to meet death, with his head high. He would face death with courage, knowing that on September 30, he had fought a good fight. Then he would be reunited with his family members, exactly two years after they had been savagely and prematurely taken away from him. He would meet his mother Angeline, and his sisters Caroline, Joceline, and Ginette. He would be forever united with them in a place where no humans were allowed to make the rules. There would be peace and harmony. There would be no pain and no hunger. Milk and honey would be plentiful. Equality and justice would prevail for everyone to enjoy. Everything would be so beautiful.

Meanwhile, Ben-X would have to face reality and the grueling steps ahead of him. His commitment, for now, was to the living. His mission was to impede the advancement of the death squad organization and give the people a reason to celebrate. He had the skills. He had the tools. His mission was going to be a success. Sweet victory was near. "KAMPE members, get ready to meet your Maker. Your time has come."

Day 730

Ben-X was known to the members of the organization as Pradel, and had visited the KAMPE headquarters quite a few times. He had studied the location very carefully. It was an old building with a large veranda in front. A blue canopy bore witness to repeated rainy seasons and was in need of some repair. The owner had gotten his money's worth out of the relic; the house would probably look much better without it. Perhaps the owner wanted to hold on to the old style and was still nostalgic of the time when BMWs and the latest-model Toyotas would pull up late at night for parties for the VIPs of the Duvalier regime.

The building was well spread over two and half acres of land, spacious enough to accommodate the dozen or so cars that always seemed to be driving in and out of the estate. Upon entering the two-story wooden structure, the quarters offered even more possibilities. There was a large meeting room that could hold thirty people comfortably. It was used as a war room where strategies were discussed over rum and other alcoholic beverages. Most of the time, however, the leader maximo made speeches to members of his permanent captive audience. The house was so huge that one could easily enter the building, get lost in the labyrinth of rooms, and not be missed.

That night the house was more crowded than usual because there was a celebration in the making. People seemed quite excited. A few members were already drunk. Ben-X had an opportunity to take a tour of the house, and had discovered what seemed like a prison cell with massive doors secured by large bars of steel. He made sure they were empty.

Nothing seemed unusual about his outfit. Everyone was carrying some kind of bag which, most of the time, contained items like clubs and guns. Some even had grenades. One never knew when it might be necessary to create some kind of disturbance. After all, they were revolutionaries, ready to defend the country from imaginary invaders. They had to be ready at all times. No one knew what Ben-X was carrying in his backpack. No one bothered to ask. That night he was just one out of a house full of renegade soldiers. The only difference was that his target was completely different and would surely surprise the partying crowd.

The building had enough flammable material to light up the night. The large, heavy drapes would certainly contribute when it was time. By 10:30 P.M., the crowd started to thin out. Ben- X imagined it would take him about ten minutes to complete his rounds. He went to the bathroom and placed one of his ready-made bombs inside the closet, hiding the device under a wicker basket. He set the timer at twenty-eight minutes. He then proceeded to the outside patio, where he placed a second device underneath a bush, setting the timer at twenty-five minutes. He heard the heavy steps of a man coming from behind. He quickly unzipped his pants and pretended that he was urinating. The man muttered some unintelligible words. He was looking for a spot to urinate, too. Maybe he was feeling the effects of the rum. The two indoor bathrooms could not keep up with the physiological needs of the men's overactive bladders.

Ben-X quickly proceeded to his last pre-selected spot: the kitchen. The small room was empty. The refrigerator entertained a constant flow of visitors looking for one item or another. Ben-X was looking for something, too, but it wasn't food. He opened the refrigerator and removed a can of beer. In exchange, he had placed a well-wrapped package behind some leftover food. Now Ben-X was really in trouble. He needed to leave the premises without looking overly rushed. In fifteen minutes, all hell would break loose. Apocalypse was about to start.

He left the complex and walked into the night. If all went as planned, the streets of Port-au-Prince would be cleaner. Ben-X was only a block away, preparing to get on his motorcycle, when something unpredictable happened. A small fire had started in the house he had just left. The remaining people went into a panic, crying, "Fire! Fire!" They were all out in the yard. Who had started the fire? Was it pure coincidence, or was it possible that another member of the resistance might have targeted the mansion?

Ben-X was not going to stick around to figure it out. More trouble was awaiting the suddenly fright-stricken group. Ben-X sped away. He had arranged to spend a few days by Tiratine in the slums of St. Antoine. He would be safe there, and would have easy access to any information that he might need. The fire progressed rapidly in the wooden structure. A series of loud explosions awakened the sleeping neighborhood. The explosions were much larger than what would have been expected from the relatively small bombs that Ben-X had placed. Then it dawned on Ben-X. The organization must have had its own cache of ammunition on the premises. It had always been rumored that two of the group's favorite weapons were concussion and incendiary grenades. If that was the case, the group had just contributed to the success of the operation.

It was not a September 30 anniversary celebration. The destruction was total. The KAMPE main headquarters was reduced to a pile of charred wood. Ben-X had not started the fire, but he would get all the credit. The police would find the trademark red handkerchief with a penny tied up in one corner—a red "X" across the effigy. Definitely and characteristically Ben-X. This time, the leaflets read:

> Oh, you fools! Did you really believe that you have what it takes to lead this nation? Did you really believe that you could exterminate the Haitian people? KAMPE, your death squad organization will be remembered for what it really was: a group of bloodthirsty, crazed lunatics. I know every single one of you. I know all the crimes each one of you has committed. In the unlikely event that you survive tonight,

you will be pursued no matter where you go. There will be no ocean too wide to cross, no country too far. The world is too small for you to hide. Justice will be done. Haiti will never die!

Ben-X

Sirens and engine noise from the fire trucks filled up the night. The situation in Delmas 33 quickly overwhelmed the poorly trained and poorly equipped firefighters. Very little water was available, anyway. The capital city was fully awakened. It looked like a giant war scene. Many soldiers started to panic and began discharging their weapons into the air. The population remained indoors, except for a few die-hard, curious onlookers. There were always those that would brave any danger to find out what was going on. They were like *telediol*[2] reporters who were always close enough to the scene to give some semblance of credibility to a story that would be spread within minutes of any event.

The rumor that night was that a major invasion was in progress and that the army was under attack. The population cheered at the news. There were also rumors that some soldiers had thrown down their weapons and had gone into hiding. The shooting went on for hours. When the situation abated at about 7:00 A.M., the whole city was exhausted. Everyone wondered what had really happened. The shooting had been more from sheer panic, and fortunately was not targeted at anyone in particular. There was no major invasion or large-scale, all-out attack on the army. It took everyone a little time to realize that it had been a false alarm and that the army was still in full control. For the Port-au-Prince population, it had been just another sleepless and tension-filled night.

Another eventful night in the war against the people of

Haiti. A war that had started exactly 730 days before and was showing no signs of abatement. The night had been long, nerve-racking, and probably much more important in the grand scale of things than the masses would have liked to admit. However, that particular night belonged to the resistance movement. They had scored an important point in the match against the powerful army.

There were several casualties in the ranks of KAMPE. The second in command was amongst the dead. The leader maximo[3] had escaped. People like him seemed to be like cats. They seemed to have nine lives. The enemy was shaken . . . stunned once more by the determination of the population. It would take them quite some time to regroup. Maybe some people would think twice about joining KAMPE. Recruitment would slow down. Just when the coup makers thought that they had everything under control, a major blow had been delivered to them. The symbolic nature of the strike was not to be minimized. If the resistance movement could get as close to the KAMPE headquarters, no one among the coup leaders was safe. They realized it all too clearly.

The repercussions of this series of successful attacks on the coup makers had implications well beyond the borders of Haiti. The international community, which had not known how to handle the situation, needed to give serious consideration to the consequences of a popular uprising. Should the masses overthrow the coup makers, no one would be safe. All the enemies that had been long identified and catalogued would become potential targets. The strategic interest of the superpowers would be seriously jeopardized. For the friends of Haiti, the latest developments posed a serious dilemma. How could they continue to show their support for the Haitian majority who had participated in the polls, while putting a lid on their revolutionary fervor and their just fight for freedom? What if a revised version of their beloved president, a toned-down version, could be delivered to them "on the wings of the eagle?" At the same time, what if key members of the popular organization were decimated through attrition, emigration, or by physical elimination by organizations like KAMPE?

Money started to flow into non-governmental organizations under the guise of humanitarian concerns. Leaders of popular organizations were co-opted and corrupted. The departure of others was facilitated through generous allocations of scholarships and exit visas. Many jumped at the opportunities and abandoned the struggle for which they had devoted most of their lives. Without their leaders, the popular resistance stood no chance of organizing itself into a successful uprising. Now, if only the army would cooperate and accept the offer of a golden parachute into exile. Everything would be perfect. The international community would save face. The Haitian people would have to agree that the friends of Haiti had done well. The coup makers would disappear into the sunset. The president would be back in his lost *fauteuil presidentiel.*

The troublemakers were no longer a factor in the popular movement. Maybe during the next election, a more acceptable candidate would emerge and win the presidency. This plan, although auspicious, was flawed from the start. First, the army officers' sentimental attachment to Haiti and the size of the financial rewards associated with their positions had been underestimated. The officers were not going to relinquish power for some uncertain life in a country in which they risked prosecution. The army officers would have to be dislodged from their positions. Remember that former general/president who was prosecuted in a civil court in Miami and had to literally run out of the United States? The second flaw was that they had underestimated the determination and the resilience of the Haitian people. The Haitians knew exactly what they wanted, and no half-baked plan was going to lead them astray. The stage was set for armed intervention and a possible occupation of Haiti.

Then there was the Ben-X factor. How many Ben-Xs were out there? How could one man create such havoc in a country under military control? What renegade nation had been providing logistical support to Ben-X and his organization? He must have an organization behind him. How much more trouble could be expected from Ben-X? These very questions were being asked in a top-secret meeting between Haitian Army General Berthold and a regional CIA chief.

"Whether Ben-X is acting alone or not, he cannot be allowed to continue to operate like this. What kind of army are you, anyway?" asked the CIA chief. "This is embarrassing. How could one man be the cause of so much trouble?" The general was furious, seeing this remark as a blatant intrusion in the country's internal affairs. As he often did, the general decided to make a joke of the man's comments.

"Maybe if we had had enough gasoline and electricity to be able to search for Ben-X throughout the night, we would have caught him." The general was obviously referring to the embargo. They continued to throw jabs at each other for a good while until the CIA representative decided it was enough, and became more conciliatory.

"We can provide you with some help to catch this man," he declared. General Berthold's pride would not allow him to accept.

"No, thank you; we will manage!"

"Well, mon commandant," said the CIA representative

with a smile, "in case you change your mind, you know what to do."

This short conversation would mark a complete change in the army's strategy toward Ben-X. A thirty-man unit was assigned to the task of collecting information about Ben-X. The unit was placed under the command of a full-fledged colonel who reported directly to General Berthold. Random searches were conducted throughout the city. Streets were frequently closed and passengers were asked to produce identification. Suspicious characters were detained for a short while and then released. The St. Antoine neighborhood, where Ben-X was hiding, was raided twice. Both times Ben-X escaped by pure luck. Every day the efforts to catch him were becoming more intense. Undercover agents seemed to be everywhere.

It was becoming more and more difficult for Ben-X to hide. Not that the army knew exactly for whom they were looking. At least that was what Ben-X believed. Various profiles were distributed throughout the city. None of them seemed to be close to reality. The population repeated its old tricks and flooded the police with false sightings. It took the army some time to realize the skullduggery of a very resourceful population. Several people were caught for making false reports and were arrested. Some of them were so savagely beaten that they lost their hearing.

As far as Ben-X was concerned, he considered his mission accomplished. He had carefully examined the dossiers of several of the perpetrators and had followed them very closely. He had even witnessed some of them performing criminal acts. He had found them guilty and had applied justice. His mission, for now, was over. However, the struggle of the people continued, since the enemy of the people was still in command.

A greater danger loomed on the horizon. One day, the

free nations of the world would have to forcefully intervene to put an end to the genocide being perpetrated in Haiti. Afterward, would the Haitian leaders be ready to lead the country out of the abyss of death? Would there be a commitment to help Haitians establish a society based on respect for the law? Would it be another 1915 when, under the pretext of bringing civilization to the black nation, Haitians were treated like sub-humans by a then overtly racist American government?

Anyone who was willing to step in and put an end to the suffering of the Haitian people would be welcomed by the masses. Two years of relentless killing were extremely difficult for anyone to bear, no matter how strong the population might be. But would the liberators turn into unwanted guests? Would it be merely a change from Haitian masters and tormenters to international masters and tormenters? Would the invaders be peacemakers and country builders, or would they be ambassadors of depravation and perversion? Would the yearning of the people for true and durable democracy be answered? Would the cycle continue indefinitely?

The position of the popular organizations seemed clear. Haiti had to lose its dependence on imperialist countries. The state had to fulfill its responsibilities vis-à-vis the wretched and the poor, and allow them to live as normal human beings. The Haitian people's aspirations for liberty and justice were rooted in the Declaration of Independence. Yet they have remained a dream thanks to the massive conspiracy among the imperialist countries, the bourgeoisie, and the reactionary army constructed by the racist invaders of 1915. Would it be a society based on justice, or would the people be coerced into an unworkable reconciliation?

Ben-X knew that the international community was designing a plan to invade Haiti. He knew it would not be for altruistic reasons. It would be to impose their own views of a democratic society on the sovereign island nation. If he had his choice, Ben-X would have liked to have watched the process, and help the country on its long road to recovery and healing. This option did not seem at all possible. It was time for Ben-X to fold again.

It was time for Ben-X to gracefully pull the curtain and take a bow. He had been kissed by death many times and then pushed aside. Maybe death had not liked the bitterness in its mouth. Ben-X had rendezvoused with death on a momentous day in September 1991. It was supposed to have been a family affair, but he was left behind for some unknown reason. He later embarked on a boat with a one-way ticket to Death City, and found himself alone on a foreign beach in a land where opportunities were supposed to be plentiful. He had traveled with modern-day pirates, toying with death every moment of the long journey into the lion's den. Death had not wanted to claim him. He had stared Death in the eyes in Carbaret, and Death had blinked. He had confronted the killer of his family and, like David did to Goliath, he challenged Death to a duel. The modern-day Goliath was no match for his determination or his hand grenades. He went into the belly of the beast, where the plans were made to maim and torture innocent people. Death had been forever present. Like a poisoned prey, he was spit out. Death was the host to many. Death met with many. Ben-X was left off the guest list. He had come so close so many times, and each time he managed to survive. The simple fact that he lived to reach his mid-forties was phenomenal. Like his fellow Haitians, he had overcome monumental obstacles. He could have died from malnutrition or some childhood infectious disease, but he had survived. He could have succumbed to the mistreatment and the psychological abuse of Mrs. Racine, his modern slave-owner. He had escaped her, too. He had beaten all the odds. He was in good health, but his heart was full of chagrin. He saw no end to the tribulations of his country. It would take the spirit of Bois-Caïman to unite the people. It would take an ideological revival to lead the people away from the brink of annihilation. The only thing left for him to do was to challenge Death itself.

Notes

1. "Behead all white men and set their houses on fire."
2. By word of mouth.
3. Supreme leader.

39

A Hero Has Fallen . . .

Ben-X roamed the streets of Port-au-Prince in an old 1981 green Chevy station wagon. Any time there was a report of a dead body on the street, he would find his way to the scene. He carried a blanket to cover their faces. At times, he seemed to be offering a prayer. He went through his rituals in a very systematic way and moved on to the next viewing. Ben-X always dressed in somber clothing and had the appearance of a *pe savan-n*[1] minus the prayer book. What was he looking for? Was he trying to get some tips from the dead people on how to get to the other side? Had he simply lost his mind? After all that he had been through, it was possible. Was he looking for the lost souls of his comrades who had fallen? How many people could endure so many losses and yet conserve all of their senses? No. Ben-X was not a deranged man. But he was up to something. It would not take long to find out.

It had been a week since Ben-X had started his new hobby. He heard that the body of a man in his early forties was lying on a pile of garbage somewhere in midtown. The man apparently had been shot the night before and had been transported there. Would the killing ever end? No one seemed to know who the man was; his body was still lying on the street with several bullet wounds.

Ben-X had a plan. Whoever the killer was, he had just

provided Ben-X with an essential tool to set this plan into motion. It would work. It had to work. Ben-X arrived at the scene and went through his usual routine. This time, however, he took an added interest in the cadaver. He took a large cover out of the station wagon and carefully wrapped the body as he cried, "Oh, Jules, my brother, what have they done to you?" Ben-X seemed inconsolable. He seemed to be stricken by grief. Certainly anyone watching the scene would think so. For Ben-X, it was just the first in a series of necessary steps to bring his plan to fruition. He had gone over every detail several times in his head and was confident everything would go very smoothly.

Individuals involved with the Haitian criminal investigation system were not very swift. Their method had always been to torture their suspect until he or she told them whatever they wanted to hear. Torture would be of no use to the army, because no one knew of Ben-X's plans. Ben-X drove straight to the small house that had been his main base since his return to the country. Most of the material obtained from the St. Philomene had been transported and kept there. Ben-X thought it was quite safe to keep everything there. Soon he would put whatever he had left in terms of explosives and ammunition to good use.

Ben-X linked all the dynamite sticks in a chain around the walls of the house. He unwrapped the dead body and positioned it by one of the windows facing the street. He positioned the body so that the man was sitting on a chair with an Uzi in his hand. Should the soldiers start shooting, the man was likely to receive new bullet wounds. The forensic department at the *Hôpital de L'Université D'Etat* had long stopped performing autopsies on bullet-ridden bodies. Ben-X's typewriter and samples of the leaflets he had left at the scene of his executions were strewn about the place for everyone to see, should there be some kind of police investigation. Red handkerchiefs were all over the room. He also placed on the coffee table a handful of red pennies with a red "X" across the effigy.

The scene for the final chapter was set. That evening would be the night on which Ben-X would make his final exit. He was satisfied that he had taken the struggle as far as one man could have possibly taken it. The limited mission he had set for himself had been accomplished. Wherever they were, his family members could rest in peace. Their brutal and untimely deaths had been avenged. At least for them, justice had been done. Still, Ben-X felt very uneasy—he was not a happy man. For millions of Haitians, the quest for freedom and justice still remained an unattainable dream. Whenever they seemed to have a glimmer of hope, some unforeseen event would take it away from them. Ben-X knew all along the struggle of the Haitian people was well beyond the reach of a one-man army, but sometimes the enemy needed to be told in very clear and unequivocal ways that every Haitian could become part of an army whose courage and bravery would be unstoppable. An army, unlike the current one that had long sold its soul, that would assist the people in their pursuit of freedom.

But now it was time for Ben-X to leave the scene. The forces of good would continue to fight and eventually would prevail over the forces of evil. The time had come for him to tip his hat in reverence to the courage of the Haitian people and say, "*Adios! Au revoir! Na we pita*. See you later!" Ben-X went to a public telephone and called the Police Headquarters.

"I want to speak to the commander," he said in a calm voice.

"Who is this?" the *officier du jour* inquired.

"Never mind who this is. I don't think your commander will appreciate it when I tell him that you did not want to hear information about Ben-X."

"Hold on!" said the officer. The commanding officer was summoned to the phone at once.

"This is Lieutenant Colonel Franklin!"

"I know where Ben-X is, right this minute!"

"Is this some kind of joke?" said the lieutenant colonel in a serious tone.

"No, mon commandant, it is not a joke. He is at Impasse Mt. Carmel number 35, the last house on the block with the mango tree in front." Click.

Before the commander could ask any more questions, Ben-X hung up. He was sure that the army would act on the information. He had probably been taped, anyway. All that Ben-X had to do now was to wait. He did not have to wait long. Less than half an hour later, a massive military operation was under way. There were truckloads of soldiers and policemen, together with some uniformed men rushing to the address. Soldiers were in transit. All the main roads were blocked. The inhabitants of the sparsely populated area were asked to evacuate the area, or at least to stay indoors until further notice. The commander, himself, was in charge of the operation. There were marksmen on top of roofs with their rifles pointed at house number 35.

The commander switched on his megaphone and ordered, "Ben-X, you are surrounded! Come out with your hands up! No harm will come to you." There was no answer. The commander was more forceful. "Ben-X! We know that you are in there. You have thirty seconds!" Again, no answer.

The commander raised his hands and gave the order to shoot. Automatic weapons blazed into the night, riddling the walls of the house with bullets. One of the soldiers pointed a grenade launcher at the glass window. He should not have done that. A huge explosion rocked the evening and blew the wall of the house into pieces, sending flaming projectiles everywhere. The soldiers instinctively ran for cover. The neighborhood remained illuminated for quite some time.

"What the . . . ?" the commander exclaimed.

The tin roof of the one-story compound was no match for the powerful explosion. It shattered like a glass windshield, sending thousands of pieces into the suddenly awakened neighborhood. The whole stage barely lit by the remaining fires seemed surreal. As the soldiers were scouring through the debris for evidence, their shadows projected on the ground, giving them the appearance of giant monsters. Every motion, every step taken by these actors looked awfully labored and mechanical. It was as if the stage director was holding a slow-motion camera, carefully documenting the moments, afraid to miss any details from the finishing scenes of this epic before the final curtain falls. Some were holding pieces of red handkerchiefs in their hands. Some were examining coins with Ben-X's characteristic marks. Others were attempting to decipher the writings on half-burnt pamphlets. In the southeast corner of the room, the blue and red Haitian flag stood, majestic, and unscathed. What could be the meaning of this flag standing amongst the ruins of what used to be "Impasse Mt. Carmel No. 35?" Was it there to bear witness to these momentous events? Or was it simply there to herald the struggle ahead and the survival of the beleaguered nation?

Suddenly, there was a cheer.

"Commandant Franklin, I think we got him!" exclaimed a soldier. He pointed to the body parts and the Uzi. What was left of the body was collected in a body bag. The commander could not contain his excitement and rushed to the television station to broadcast the news. It came right from the horse's mouth: Ben-X was officially dead . . . . The police file read:

Case no. 0002875
Name: Ronald Benjamin St. Fort (aka Ben-X)
Age: Approximately 41
Cause of death: Multiple wounds by explosive missiles
Status: SOLVED

Pour qui sonne le glas? For whom were they tolling the knell? At the top of a hill about a half a mile away, a man in his early forties watched the whole scene with a grin on his face. Would the bell toll again? What would be the next call to duty?

Ode to a Fallen Hero . . .
Over hills and valleys he leaps,
His heart full of sorrow
His courage is that of a rhino
He is our Ben-X; he is our hero
Injustice he could not stand
The wretched and the poor he embraced
His humble origins he could not forget
He is our Ben-X; he is our hero
Equality and justice for all
Is his motto
Always passionate and loving
Magnanimous and altruistic, he stands
He is our Ben-X; he is our hero
He knows no fear
Like an African warrior,
Relentless, he hunts his enemies
He is our Ben-X; he is our hero
He is gone but not forgotten

Tomorrow, 6,000,000 Ben-Xs will rise
To carry the flag of our struggle
Equality and justice are our dream
The people's fight must go on . . . .

Note

1. Self-declared priest.

Epilogue

A Year Later . . .

For the battered and exhausted Haitian people, deliverance came in the form of the most expensive and largest military operation in the country's 200-year history. A twenty-three-vessel armada from the U.S. Navy was stationed off the coast, ready to storm the capital city with deadly missiles. A three-man mission composed of an ex-president, a charismatic black general, and the chairman of the powerful U.S. Senate Armed Services Committee attempted a last-ditch effort to convince the military rulers to take their loot and run to avoid a bloodbath.

Out of Fort Bragg, North Carolina, the 82nd Airborne Division was ordered into battle. Destination: Haiti. The U.S. president who, in an unusually late chat a few days before, had outlined a long list of crimes committed by the Haitian Army had previously set the tone. With his credibility on the line and the 1996 presidential election in mind, military intervention in Haiti was ordered by the commander in chief. What is a president supposed to do when he is pressured from all sides to resolve a crisis that his country had started in the first place? Anyway, if the aim of the coup makers had been to take the wind out of the popular movement and to make the deposed president more agreeable, one could safely say that the coup had been a resounding success. The men from Washington would have their cake and eat it, too. Operation "Restore Democracy" was about to begin. It was very weak in comparison to the kind of democratic movement that the popular organizations had always fought for. Like Ben-X, they had no choice but to fold.

In the pre-dawn hours of September 19, 1994, the sky over the Caribbean was transformed into the theater of an apocalyptic scene. Hundreds of service support aircraft, Huey, Cobra, Chinook, and other Army helicopters, were flying low toward the main targets. The cheering crowds could finally let out their joy. *"Mise-ya fini pou nou!"* (Long live the Americans!) There was no resistance. The *Cacos*[1] movements of the early years of the century were not resuscitated. All the talk about the Haitian Army having taken to the mountains to organize guerilla warfare had been pure hogwash. The hit list widely discussed amongst the coup supporters was not pursued. No assets were spared to make the mission a friendly but firm takeover. America could not afford any casualties. Back on capitol Hill, members from both sides of the aisle watched as the situation unfolded.

Once again, Haiti, the first black republic of the world, was a nation in tutelage. The demands of the people stood no chance of ever being heard. When was the last time the United States was on the side of the masses? They had had many opportunities in the past, and they had not seized them. They certainly were not going to start with Haiti, the poorest country in the hemisphere. For the Haitian masses, it was back to the drawing board. The saga would continue. The never-ending fight for democracy was put on hold. The masses were well aware that true democracy could not come wrapped as a gift on the wings of a bald eagle. The chaos was likely to continue for generations to come in the beleaguered nation. One could hear the people singing in unison:

Guinin yan desan-n
yo pote you fos ki ban nou libete
Guinin yan desan-n
yo pote you fos ki ban-n libete
Libete ki Libere, libete ki delivre
He, libete se pran pou-n pran-l
He, libete se pran pou-n pran-l
Se pou ou pran-l ak tout ke-ou
Se nou plan-l aK tout nan-m nou
Pa gade sou lot, Pa gade sou lot
Pou ban-nou Libete
(Boukman Eksperyans)

The spirit (Guinin) came down
They brought a force that gave us freedom
Freedom that frees, freedom that delivers
Freedom, you have to take it (yourself) with all your heart
Freedom you have to take it (yourself) with all your soul
Do not count on others
Do not count on others to give you freedom
(Boukman Eksperyans)

Note

1. Guerilla movement during American Occupation.